Timeless Writings 39

Different Writers
2017-18

Tatay Jobo Elizes
Compiler
January 2018

Published by Tatay Jobo Elizes, Self-Publisher

This book is published and printed under the expressed permission of the various authors compiled for this purpose of making their articles and essays available to the public and promote reading among Filipinos, young and old. They own the copyrights to their writings. Authors can ask to withdraw their writings here anytime and will be edited out in next printing. Printing of this book is using the present day method of Print-On-Demand (POD) system, where prints will never run out of copies. Authors are free to republish or reprint with other publishers and printers anytime.

ISBN Codes

ISBN – 13: 978 – 1725566422 and
ISBN – 10: 1725566427

Disclaimer: Views are expressed by the authors alone. Tatay Jobo Elizes does not knowingly publish false information and may not be held liable for the views of the authors exercising their right to free expression.

Self-Publisher's Details:

Contact: job_elizes@yahoo.com
Website: http:tinyurl.com/mj76ccq
www. tatayjoboelizes.webs.com

Contents

ooooo

1
When Harry Met Rody

Rene Saguisag
Dateline, Nov. 1, 2017, Opinion
Manila Times Column

Our newspapers should have someone like Linda Greenhouse of the New York Times, when reporting or commenting on an item with a legal dimension.

Too often, local media for instance mis-report a motion for reconsideration (before the same court) as an appeal (to a higher court.)

Even legal thriller novelist John Grisham, a lawyer who writes so well, might need a tighter editor. I have enjoyed in particular his novels with a sports angle, such as Calico Joe (baseball, 2012) and Playing for Pizza (American pro football, 2007). I was incredulous to see John seemingly commit what we here often do: "The fact that [quarterback] Rick was now a fugitive added a level of daring and romance that the Italians found irresistible. In a country where laws are flaunted and those who flaunt them are often glamorized, the pursuit by the police was the dominant topic whenever two or more [Parma] Panthers got together." At 221, paperback. It seems to me "flaunted", often misused here, should be "flouted". But, who am I to correct a native English speaker who writes so well?*

"Subornation of perjury" is to induce to perjure. But, a statement attributed to a Supreme Court Justice' s staff supposedly stated "subordination or perjury." Phil. Star, Oct. 27, 2017,

p. 2, col. 4. *Susmariano po naman! Typo po malamang.* I am incredulous that such a high-level staff would commit such an egregious lapse.

A newspaper' s copy reader or ombudsman should also ban any further misstatement that Ferdinand E. Marcos was born on September 11, 1917. It should be 1916. I have a copy of his birth certificate, affirming what he said under oath in a Honolulu court in 1986, as I recall it. Kim Lumagbas, a San Beda Alabang Law stude of mine produced Macoy's birth certificate, echoed by seven others. ABS-CBN should get part of the credit for publishing that fact in 1998, thanks to Melvin dela Cuesta. Indeed, if anyone can show me a Macoy birth certificate carrying 1917, I will eat it.

The Philippine Postal Corporation has to be probed by the Ombudsman, Department of Justice and the Commission on Audit for falsifying history and wasting government funds on a commemorative stamp for the kleptocrat/human rights violator. 2017 is not his centennial, but his 101st birth anniversary. Next time I visit the burial ground of my late father-in-law in Libingan ng Mga Bayani, I just may consider trying to go visit Apo's resting place and see if the epitaph says: HERE A LAWYER LIES STILL, found in an Irish cemetery.

The destruction of our values, institutions and processes Macoy accelerated in the 60's-80's, following World War II, when we still had vestiges of old-fashioned delicadeza and palabra de honor, which ruination continues full blast today. Let's hope new presidential spokesperson Harry Roque will demonstrate a better command of language than Meyor/Prez Rody himself, Martin Andanar and Sal Panelo, with their rather constipated vocabulary.

Thus, the regrettable resort to kabastusan. Too bad urbane Ernesto Abella had to be let go. No room for the non-lawyer's urbanidad. Now, a Digong, Jr., sa kahambugan? But, I hope Harry regards me as a friend; recall Napoleon advising not to disrupt an enemy making a mistake.

I was candidate, Prez-elect and Prez Cory's echo and I would tell the Palace Brat Pack, "that is what I was told to say, I am not allowed to think here, puede ba, next question," and we'd would move on. Brilliant creative Teddy Boy Locsin, another presidential echo, was on his own when he made the inelegant "You' re No. 1" gesture with his right middle finger. Muy pillo.

Cory had breeding and elegance, previously required or expected of our officials, particularly high ones. (I made her lose her temper only once, when I remarked early December 1989, at the height of a coup, that Senate Prez Salonga was right: there was a perception of her double captivity, by the military and the U.S.; when I got home, my wife at once barked, "ano yung itinawag ni Cory that between her and Uncle Jovy, atbp."; double captivity I was in, by two women I cherished.) Mar Roxas got it when once he used "PI!" That Digong is not getting it for far cruder lingo galore suggests we may be decaying faster than seems possible. The Cycle is Savagery, Civilization and Decay.

Sticks and stones may break my bones but words can never hurt me? But, words can hurt too, and the new presidential mouthpiece is shopping for hollow blocks, to throw at us, making us cower in fear. We are cowards pretending not to be so.

If a farmer, after failing to get justice for a daughter raped by an hacendero, throws a stone at the system, I am incredulous that Harry says to throw a hollow block at the peasant. Many who join the NPA are poor, with unredressed grievances, as the law too often represents the biases of the ruling classes. I am glad that mercurial Digong could sound more conciliatory, last we heard.

A Senator was quoted here last Sunday to say "senators won't allow suspects to invoke their right to against self-incrimination without a valid reason." Our Constitution does not work in the Senate? "Valid reason" enough for me, the human and constitutional right not to speak. It seems to me suspects can just cite the Bill of Rights (Artikulo III, name of our new lawyers' group). Most any lawyer's first advice to any suspect is to "shut up," which the Constitution protects, while the attorney tries to build the strongest possible defense under the laws of the land.

To entice a suspect to talk, not to his own perdition, he should be offered effective immunity which only a court, I believe, can grant. The legislative Committee on a proper vote should go to some court which would cooperate as a co-worker in government, the U.S. praxis. Congress cannot usurp a judicial function in exempting one from prosecution.

Yes, where in the Constitution is Congress given the power to detain because someone is not aiding it in doing its job - legislation? What law does the Senate have in mind that they now need the aid of harassed terrorized and bullied laymen anyway? Intimidation and terrorism our public servants should shy away from. Forgetting purposes is the most common form of innocence, to paraphrase Nietzsche. Guests or resource persons should never be identified by the Senate as "suspects" ;, more proper in a police stationhouse, where the mantra begins with, "you have a right to remain silent, ..."?

The Justice Secretary should not usurp the judicial function of a court in granting immunity, either. He can only ask some court, not impose on it, per Sec. 7 of Rule 119 of the Rules of Court.

Lawmakers and Cabinet Members should study, instead of joining us in having to spend too much time in traffic, taking pixes/selfies and watching basketball games where we cannot be world-class and have to import players and even coaches. *Josme po naman*. What time is left for productive effort seen in the progressive countries?

This is 2017, not the middle ages or the period of cruel Inquisition. Lawmakers should legislate for our people, and not flagellate, guests.

For instance, last week an "exclusive club" admitted me (with two others). When I asked for the check, I saw it was for P1,800.00. I tendered P2,000.00, in cash. It was rejected, along with my senior citizen' s card (and only a credit card would do). Paging Romy Macalintal. Is remedial legislation needed on what is meant by "legal tender" in exclusive plutocratic enclaves where I obviously don't belong? Congress should study my plaint.

Romy and I wish our pal, Harry Roque, well, in the bowels of labyrinthine serpentine Malacañang. We count on him having a broader vocabulary than what Digong Duterte, Sal Panelo and Mart Andanar have shown so far. Harry should say whoa, whoa to our *napakadaldal na Pangulo. Be real, not plastic. Huwag magtaksil sa kanyang kauri.*

I am reminded of the film When Harry Met Sally; there, Meg Ryan moaned and faked an orgasm in a resto, prompting another woman to tell the waiter she wanted whatever Meg had ordered. (There was a town known as Sexmoan in Pampanga, now Sasmuan).

Teka, teka, this is a family newspaper nga pala. Our family's Undas is on the 8th, next week, when I mark a decade of my being an Unmerry Widower. No gridlock, or less, by then, when we will troop to Manila Memorial. I believe it was Gen. Mon Farolan who more than once wisely suggested that we go on birth or death anniversaries, instead of overcrowding on November 1.

Tradition? As I recall reading in Selecciones de Reader's Digest decades ago, a tradition is a social vice that has become incurable (*la tradicion es un vicio social que se ha vuelto incurable*). Undas in my youth in Pasig we associated with stealing chickens. Now, larceny could be for purloining P50M, less a thou, for bailable graft, instead of non-bailable plunder, for Digong's frat brods. But, of course innocence is presumed, save apparently in Congress and Malacañang, the graveyard of the Bill of Rights for critics, who should now ready themselves for Harry's hollow blocks.

What a hollow blockhead Halloween idea for governance. But, I support Digong on the Balangiga Bells. Also, on the Bangsamoro Basic Law, and here Senator Leila joins us. Kudos, Lei, for deserving the "Prize for Freedom" , a feat you share with Prez Cory, who told me in December 1989, "from now on, things won't be hunky-dory," and proceeded to make sumbong to my ever-loving Dulce.

See you on the 8th, my luv.

ooooo

2
Lack of Inter-Branch Courtesy; Answering to History

Rene Saguisag
Dateline, Nov 8, 2017,
Manila Times Opinion Column

As spokesperson of then candidate Cory Aquino in 1985-86, it was a pleasant task for me to announce that Manang Letty Ramos-Shahani, then in the foreign service, had come out openly in support of our candidate, in defiance of the dictator. Then came the equally public and bold defection of Col. Mariano Santiago, a hero in Edsa'86. I was reminded of him because his brother, General Dionisio had just resigned/retired or fired as PDEA chief. Running in the family is high principle, at stake in a pending impeachment proceeding.

I endorsed another candidate for Chief Justice (CJ) in 2012, not Associate Justice Meilou Sereno. But, the President' s call was for her, which was legit and totally in order. So unlike the gross post-midnight appointment of her predecessor, which called for institutional correction, by the people, thru their Representatives, done via impeachment, and by their Senators, via conviction and removal.

Now, courtesy seems to be in very short supply in this mal-administration. *So bastos! La cortesia no quita la valentia,* the Palace should remember. Courtesy does not detract from valor.

Every Justice, among many many others, has his moist eye cast on the Chief Justiceship, so I can understand the seeming lack of intramural support. But, it is not only the institution but the country itself at stake.

I am incredulous at the rate Harry Roque arguably appears to be self-destructing. For him, and not say, remarkable Sal Panelo, to say CJ Meilou must resign so as not to damage the Supreme Court, sounds bizarre. What about the damage to the country' s institutional arrangements by such egregious lack of inter-departmental courtesy?

So, here's another stone, from where I sit, but I rightly don't know whether Harry will go to a hollow block factory or a bakery. Santa banana! Not satisfied with speaking for the Philippines, he now seems to speak also for China and its intentions. By what authority naman kaya? If he can really speak for China, he might find some way for it to stop exporting shabu to the Philippines. We watch what others do, not what they say. Does China really insist on using its labor force in its infrastructure projects here with our high unemployment? While making us stop doing what we want in our very own?

Even more, or equally, startling is UP Manila's opposition to medical marijuana, echoing the Philippine Medical Association. They may assume that the U.S., Canada, and many countries in South America and Europe are insane not to oppose marijuana. Bill Clinton, Dubya Bush and Barack Obama all flirted with Mary Jane, which may explain why Bill, as sexual predator, later romanced Moooannniiicccaa Lewinsky.

What an individual does to destroy himself, with marijuana, the state would take over, by imprisoning, in some stinking overcrowded jail, and stigmatizing, a user, for life or a loooong time.

Portugal has decriminalized all drugs and sees users as sick frail people to be saved and rehabbed, not criminals to be destroyed by a prison record. But, things seem normal enough there. After an initial spike in use 15 or so years ago, it went down. And I have friends who went to Fatima last month, to mark the centennial of our Lady's Apparition in Portugal. Antonio Guterres is the new SecGen of the UN, where its General Assembly Special Session on drugs is moving towards liberalization.

Our Catholic Church supports medical marijuana use to deal with suffering.

Decriminalizing should kill the syndicates because the state will supply for free, or at nominal cost, in rehab facilities what syndicates charge in humongous sums. Kill the profit motive and kill trafficking.

China can prove its friendship by knocking off its shabu supply source. A small price to pay for our virtual dishonorable surrender of West Philippine Sea.

Last Tuesday, San Sebastian surrendered honorably to San Beda. I got to watch the game for all the NCAA semifinal marbles at the Mall of Asia Arena. Initially, I was seated at the Baste side. I had on a yellow shirt (Baste's color) and a red jacket**** (San Beda's). Then I was moved to courtside.

San Beda outlasted San Sebastian, which fought gallantly, and the Lions will now face the Lyceum juggernaut.

I missed our Indian Yell that whips the blood and our former rousing Victory Song. I still feel antsy as to why the losers are made to stay on court and sing. They should be allowed to go at once to their locker room, and let alone to weep, in privacy.

Attendance was all right last Tuesday but the title series which begins today, in Araneta, another planet which is farther, and I cannot go to, I fear. I live in Palanan and the other night, for a meeting in Conti's in Greenbelt, nearly two hours it took me. This is where the administration&# 39;s Kill-Pa-More policy may be needed, which seems to be overdoing it in the messy bloody and failed drug war. Take-Prisoners- for-Rehab will do.

No incident, much less a rhubarb or donnybrook, marred last Tuesday' s NCAA offering. Commissioner Bai Cristobal and the three refs deserve kudos. Two years ago, when San Beda lost to Letran, 82-85, in overtime. in the final game, the Three Blind Mice didn't see a lane violation with seconds to go. But, that's all right. San Beda owes it to one and all to remind them from time to time that it is not the only team in the league.

And Robert Bolick, like Jerry West in the 1970 NBA Finals, made an even longer shot from the foul line, a buzzer-beater, last Tuesday; without it, the score would have been a close 73-71. More than worth the price of admission. (OK, I had a free ducat.)

Looming is another Thrilla.

PNoy is charged in the Sandiganbayan for Mamasapano, an operation that bagged Marwan, who had at least $5M on his head. No one runs for Prez claiming perfection and infallibility. Else, only the likes of Bedan Justice Gregorio Perfecto would qualify. When troopers go to enemy lair, particularly Morolandia, they knew some would come back in boxes.

Kennedy and the Bay of Pigs, Johnson and the Tet Offensive, Carter and the Iran rescue, Reagan and the Marines in Beirut, the Bushes and Obama in Iraq, and Clinton in Black Hawk Down, might have erred and misjudged, but with no personal gain. To err is human.

And like Fidel Castro, proclaim, "la historia me absolvera!" ** History will absolve me, PNoy can say. Indeed, the like the American Presidents, he should not have even been charged.

There is no talk even of going after those who killed comrades in fatal friendly fire in Marawi. Nor of why Digong was in Russia when the Marawi bloodletting began. And rightly so even if military intelligence again surfaced as a seeming contradiction in terms. *Sino po ang mga natulog sa pansitan,* resulting in having to destroy Marawi in order to save it? Like Vietnam' s Ben Tre?

Graft in PNoy's situation is hard to fathom. Usurpation? What, pray tell, is a Prez and Commander-in- Chief, prohibited from doing within his executive domain?

Saguisag & Associates Lawyers 4045 Bigasan Street, Palanan 1235 Makati Office Nos. (+632) 551-6350/833-4140 Fax No. (+632) 831-2276

ooooooo

3
Major Defect of Tax Reform: It Will Promote Economic Inequality

Marcelo L. Tecson
Dateline, November 9, 2017,
WFA yahoogroup

The major defect of the government's tax reform is not just in what is IN it—it will OVERTAX 'til it hurts the POOR — but more so in what is NOT in it: it will NOT similarly OVERTAX 'til it hurts the RICH, therefore it is PRO-RICH and discriminatory to the POOR! IT IS A SUBTLE PROMOTER OF GLOBALLY LAMENTED UNDEMOCRATIC ECONOMIC TYRANNY OFTHE MINORITY RICH OVER THE MAJORITY POOR: GROSS WEALTH & INCOME INEQUALITY AS IT INCREASES THE WEALTH OF THE RICH AND WORSENS THE POVERTY OF THE POOR!

While it will reduce the income tax of the 30% income-taxpaying population, it will saturate the remaining 70% without jobs or enough income (who will not benefit from income tax reduction) with increased taxes, resulting in

(1) "CONFISCATION" through higher taxes of their meager assets used to buy consumables, or

(2) DOING WITHOUT consumption items made UNAFFORDABLE by higher taxes, hence making them POORER and more miserable. In stark contrast, it will not reduce at all the existing surplus wealth of the ultra RICH. In addition, they will

be left a hefty 65% taxed income out of their annual earnings, after paying relatively low 35% top individual income tax rate, thereby perpetuating their huge annual increase in wealth that makes them RICHER with luxurious lifestyle.

WHY WE CANNOT LEAVE EVERYTHING TO ECONOMISTS THE FALLOUT FROM ECONOMISTS WORLD WIDEMISSING THE POINT ON HOW TO ATTAIN ECONOMIC EQUALITY: THE GOVERNMENT'S TAX REFORM ENDORSED BY MANY ECONOMISTS WILL WORSEN ECONOMIC INEQUALITY—INSTEAD OF PRODUCING ECONOMIC EQUALITY— BECAUSE IT AIMS AT ECONOMIC GROWTH, NOT AT EQUITABLE SHARING OF GROWTH BETWEEN RICH AND POOR.

The government's Tax Reform for Acceleration and Inclusion (TRAIN) is aimed at fast and inclusive economic growth shared between the POOR and the RICH. Unfortunately, TRAIN will produce the opposite—not the desired—effect, because it will not help attain inclusive growth that will address the following gross income inequality expressed as shares in economic growth:

"Cielito Habito…former economic planning minister, told AFP… that in 2011 the Philippines' 40 richest families on the Forbes wealth list accounted for 76 percent of the country's gross domestic product (GDP) growth." (Agence France-Presse, "Philippines' elite swallow country's new wealth," Inquirer Business Online, March 3, 2013).

In 2014, the "country's 50 richest individuals …earned $8.45 billion—that's equivalent to 51% of the GDP growth ($16.6 billion)." (Paolo Taruc, "A tale of two economies: Exclusive growth in the

Philippines," CNN Phil., September 21, 2015). The goal of TRAIN, fast economic growth, is crucial, but as key to economic equality it is fallacious because equality is not solely dependent on growth. Economic equality is about equitable sharing of economic growth or income—which translates to equitably shared wealth—between the RICH and POOR. Whether the growth is one percent or ten percent is of no moment, what matters is the proportionate share of the POOR in it. Economic growth that creates job for the POOR does not result in economic equality. While the RICH corner bulk of growth, the POOR's compensation from growth-created jobs is not even enough for their basic necessities: food, clothing, shelter, education, and health care. To the POOR masses without taxable income who will not benefit from income tax reduction but will bear raised consumption taxes, their case will be from bad to worse. As proponents of TRAIN will not raise their 35% proposed top individual income tax rate for the RICH to our recommended 50% or higher top income tax rate—with the resulting increased tax collection suggested to be used in economic development and poverty reduction programs—TRAIN will not address gross wealth and income inequality in our midst.

JUST WHY ARE WE HELPLESS INMINIMIZING THE GLOBALLY LAMENTED PROBLEM OF LACK OF INCLUSIVE GROWTH, GROSS WEALTH AND INCOME INEQUALITY, OR THE RICH GETTING RICHER AND THE POOR POORER? IF THERE IS A PROBLEM, IT IS MAN-MADE— IT IS THE LACK OF POLITICAL WILL OF GOVERNMENTS ININSTITUTING THE LEGAL, MORAL, EQUITABLE, AND EXPEDITIOUS WAY

OF DOING IT: PROGRESSIVE TAXATION WHICH CHARGES THE RICH HIGHER TAX OR PREMIUM AS PRICE FOR THEIR GREATER WEALTH AND COMFORT UNDER GOVERNMENT PROTECTION — A CLASSIC CASE OF THE GREATER THE BENEFIT THE GREATER THE PAYMENT,

We can wait 'til kingdom come but the RICH will not share their surplus wealth (some probably derived from their overpriced goods and services) to the POOR on a sustained basis. Thus, there is no alternative to having the RICH compulsorily do it through PROGRESSIVE TAXATION, which entails taking some more taxes from the abundant annual income of the RICH (but not from their existing wealth) and spending the increase in taxes for economic development and poverty reduction. If for national interest the government can sacrifice the one and only one priceless and irreplaceable LIFE of every Filipino SOLDIER who died in MARAWI, why can't it similarly sacrifice a dispensable part of the abundant, surplus, and clearly replaceable multi-million-peso—or billion-peso—MONEY of the ultra RICH through increased income taxation for the same national interest?

MARCELO L. TECSONA CPA and Concerned Citizen C/o San Juan and Associates27S Midland Manor 2Ortigas AvenueGreenhills, San Juan City 1500 November 9, 2017

Oooooo

4
Revgov? Impeachment Blues

Rene Saguisag
Dateline, Nov. 23, 2017,
Manila Times Opinon Columns

Chief Justice (CJ) Art Panganiban, in his typically edifying November 19, 2017 column, along with many other constitutional scholars, seems to assume casually that the removal of Marcos in 1986, was not in accord with the 1973 Constitution.

The 1973 Constitution I call Siopao; the barangays were said to have been convened, and asked who wanted Siopao - almost all attendees raised their hands. The Comelec tallied the raised hands as "Yes." I wasn't aware though of any such Assembly being held in the places I was familiar with. In any event, our Constitutions of 1935 (Art. VII, Sec. 9), 1973 (Art. VII, Sec. 9) and 1987 (Art. VII, Sec. 8) all say that a President' s term may be ended by "removal from office."

The People "removed" Marcos in 1986, to local and world acclaim. Erap was "removed" in 2001, at which the world, puzzled, looked askance, but which "removal" arguably, was not unconstitutional, on the basis of the constitutional language. However, the Supreme Court (SC) instead ruled that he had resigned, on the weird basis of somebody else's diary. Baffling to the outside world and to certain of us, natives. But, "removal" could have led to a Revolutionary Government (RevGov) and the wise Justices may find themselves jobless, as in 1986. Hence, resignation, as one theory.

Erap's lawyers (I wasn't one of them yet) had prudently advised that he write to the Senate Prez and the Speaker that he was stepping ASIDE due to temporary disability, not stepping DOWN. He did so and was the last one to know he had resigned kuno.

Out of power, overdog-turned-underdog Erap renewed his invite that I join his legal team. I did. When I orally argued the case in the Supreme Court, there was no discussion I could recall on resignation. But, if a Justice had raised the issue of whether he was "removed" by some people and the military, in the same way we removed Marcos, I might have had "little" wiggle room. But, the Justices might have realized that their own tenure might be in jeopardy.

We need a law on the procedure on resignations, to clarify such issues as to who Comelec Chair Andy Bautista should have submitted his resignation. In the U.S., Nixon submitted his letter to the Secretary of State, as explicitly provided by 3 U.S Code Sec. 20.

My attempts to have such a local clarifying law did not get anywhere in the 1987-92 Senate. It's time someone in the legislature should start the process of filling up the lacuna. But, it seems the lawmakers would rather probe in aid of something and impeach, also in aid of something and I fret about the way Congress expects a guest to check the Bill of Rights at the door. It is said that a lawyer who defends himself has a fool for a client, as the House well knows, which it should factor in. (And, do the solons and others have to eat in the session hall? *Ten am pa lang the other day. . . .*)

Impeachment may lead to the capital penalty of removal and the target should be given every leeway. Sporting and fair was what guided a House panel in the impeachment of Federal Judge Alcee L. Hastings."It granted the defense" the extraordinary prerogative of his counsel [Terence J. Anderson] to question any of the witnesses, if he so chooses, for up to the point of 10 minutes" . Impeachment Inquiry, Hearings, Subcommittee on Criminal Justice, Pursuant to H. Res. 128, Impeaching Alcee L. Hastings, May 18, 1988, Serial No. 11, p. 8.

In my first year or so of practice, cross-examination was allowed in preliminary investigations. In one case, Manila Fiscal Serafin Cuevas allowed us, as counsel, to cross-examine. I learned a lot watching famed iconic soft-spoken Doy Quisumbing cross. Marcos removed that right, facilitating the prosecution of "subversives." Impeachment is sui generis, in a class by itself, and the House should consider allowing it, to mitigate its image as an extension of Malacañang.

CJ Meilou's basic offense, from where I sit, is asserting judicial independence, which may get in the way of a RevGov. Like Senator Leila de Lima, had she kept quiet or voted the way Digong was seen to favor, she would "most likely" not be undergoing her current ordeal. Another offense: she was seen to jump the queue - from a relatively junior Associate, to Chief - and generated sadness. (I supported another aspirant in 2012 but support her now as one legitimate CJ, which was more than I "regret to have to say for post midnight-appointee Rene Corona.)"

If her lawyers file a case in the SC, she would have to inhibit herself but it would also smoke out her fellow magistrates into recusing themselves if they would be witnesses against her, as ballyhooed.

Seniority may be sacred here but it is nothing in the U.S. Supreme Court. CJ Roberts was not even an Associate Justice when elevated. No resentment from those bypassed who may have had an understandable moist eye cast on the Chief Justiceship. (In January 1987, turned down a signed SC appointment; public service its its own reward, my mantra, and I, then 47, saw many far more deserving seniors. Non sibi sed patriae; not self, but country) Anyway, Holmes and J.B.L. Reyes, et al., are better remembered fondly than CJs, like Roger Taney, a Catholic who ruled that blacks were chattels in the 1857 Dred Scott case.

Congress is better off lawmaking and policymaking, not probing and impeaching and judging. Lavish lifestyle for getting an expensive car for court use? Eventually, all 15 should get one, state-of-the- art; on SALN, punished lightly in R.A. No. 6713, has she been given a chance to amplify or correct, if needed? CJ telling Judges not to surrender without a warrant, which document the Constitution requires? Of course it is said that impeachment is political but not to the point of making it a Kenkoy proceeding. We need to study harder the history of impeachment of magistrates in the U.S., England and even India. Only U.S.S.C. Justice Samuel Chase was impeached; impeachment failed. Chase acquitted.

ASEAN was not a failure. No occasion to blurt out, Putin Ina! Xia-pao Naman! Trumpong Kangkarot! (Our Rizal High "Rizalian" graduation issue labelled me Galawgaw.) But, its effect on traffic is something to note. No gridlocks then, which we again have, and how! This is what Digong may properly apologize for, not the MRT glitches about which he could have done nothing. Wotta lucky guy. In the San Beda-Lyceum face-off last week, as an alum of both schools, no way Digong could have lost.

Sec. Art Tugade was in Araneta and maybe chanted with us Umpa! Umpa! Beda-Beda-Beda-Fight, etc., which never fails to whip Bedan blood).

But, easy on Digong's use of addictive pain-killer Fentanyl. The Nov. 20, 2017 issue of TIME said: "[I]n 2016, the Drug Enforcement Administration (DEA) reported more than 30,000 seizures of fentanyl, a dramatic spike from the 5,000 documented in 2014. The man-made formulas are so powerful that police officers participating in drug raids where fentanyl is confiscated have overdosed simply by breathing in particles of the drug released into the air. . . . The opioid epidemic may have been sparked by prescription medications, but it's now a label for a much larger addiction crisis in the U.S., spanning dozens of drugs both legal and not." At 36-37. An old problem. Macoy's mother was arrested, suspected to have sold opium and heroin to Arellano Hi students, according to Tibo Mijares in Conjugal Dictatorship. The Marcoses were that poor then.*

Addiction and overdose may kill one but the state does not rush death in the U.S. by EJKs. "You're killing yourself by addiction, the PNP will do you a favor by EJKs," seems to be the mantra here, reducing our population by thousands. We should share the pain of addicts and their loved ones. We wish the Philippine Drug Enforcement Agency luck. Reduce population by Kill-Kill-Kill not its style.

In limiting our population, only two kids suggested but how about only one wife (and perhaps one kulasisi for each macho)? Who are our role models? Ideally, only one wife, but if kulasisis are factored in, nothing doing. Digong has a fave partner on public occasions he should marry so as not to confuse the youth, prosecutors and judges. He is reported to have kulasisis in Davao and Cagayan de Oro, per scuttlebutt. Speaker Bebot Alvarez converted to a tribe in Mindanao allowing more than one wife and famously asked who among us has no kulasisi? Are we really a nation of Lady-Killers?

I label Lady-Killers as emotional terrorists even as we label the NPAs as terrorists, but we may not properly take into account why the latter rebel. They may be citizens with a grievance, e.g., a farmer whose daughter gets raped by an hacendero, who is not prosecuted or if prosecuted, gets acquitted. The farmer may then go out of the system.

But, what is Prez Digong's excuse for going RevGov? May we have a Heal-Heal-Heal, not Kill-Kill-Kill, presidency instead?

So my mantra, the right thing must be done in the right way at the right time in the right place for the right reason. Thus - "The key to successful extramarital sex, therefore, was discretion. Mrs. Patrick Campbell, perhaps the most outspoken woman in polite Victorian society, said dryly: `It doesn't matter what you do in the bedroom, as long as you don't do it in the street and frighten the horses'. "W. Manchester, The Last Lion - Winston Spencer Churchill 74 (1974, paperback)." Here, discretion not needed, per Speaker Bebot Alvarez. Wide-open society. In decay.(?)

Digong must keep my five R's Mantra in mind. Be careful with RevGov, and maybe, faithful Honeylet deserves matrimony. Talking about Leila's guilt is improper. I am again reminded of her because Charles Manson just died at 83. Nixon blasted him as guilty of the rape-murder of pregnant Sharon Tate, and the killing of others. The public howled. The White House was quick to apologize; no, it did not mean to prejudge.

Have Digong, Sec. Vit Aguirre (another one now with a moist eye cast on the Senate) and SolGen Joe Calida talked too much about Leila's supposed guilt? Had she kept quiet, she would now be in the Senate where, with any kind of luck - I never underrate anyone's capacity for subjective growth - we may have Prez Manny Pacquiao (now bored in the Senate) shine and and go for the whole enchilada, with Veep Mocha Uson in 2022. Those concerned may all play coy but if ordered to run by Digong, who are they to say no?

Play coy, I urge, and not to say China is "privileged; to be third telcos player. Let it compete and bid. Else, if unbidden, it comes, we may feel like the Pop, who, asked for her daughter' s hand, had to say, "sure, you might as well have her hand. You have had everything else." *Pakipot muna. Hele-hele, bago quiere.*

And charge, not just shame Gen. Dionisio Santiago, so he can defend himself in some proper forum. Same fate as Sec. Mike Sueno's. The Palace convicted and shamed them without due process.

Palace, I don't like your style.

oooooo

5
Chacha in a Scofflaw Nation

Rene Saguisag
Dateline, Jan. 31, 2018
Manila Times Opinon Columns

So ex-Customs Chief Nicanor Faeldon is now a Batang City Jail (BJC) candidate-member, in Pasay. There we visited Doy Laurel midnight of February 17, 1984 when he was arrested for alleged illegal possession of a gun. Maverick Judge Dionisio Capistrano dismissed the case the next day, a Saturday. We were 42 lawyers, led by Ka Celing Muñoz Palma, Soc Rodrigo and Paddy Padilla. We argued that the gun had been planted (good that on dismissal, no one suggested that we ask for the gun's "return, " haha. Doy, a hero but, muy pillo).

I was a BCJ candidate-member myself in early 1983, in Quezon City, not good enough for ABC, Aguinaldo, Bonifacio-Bicutan and Crame. On February 4, 1983 Judge Jose Castro jailed me cuz I had allegedly "arrogantly announced that President Ferdinand E. Marcos is a super-subversive . . . ." and "this is now the second offense of contempt [I] committed" . Fined P50.00 earlier for bitching that the court was getting militarized given the presence of so many uniforms I said, "I' d gladly pay it, Your Honor," pulling out a hundred-peso bill, and asked, "may I say something more for another fifty pesos?" He changed the subject cuz I was loony even then.

There in Pasay also I visited Gina Doe in the mid-90s. She had retained me by phone patch, over

Radio Veritas, one early morning. She had been accused of mutilating John Doe, her lover who napped in their motel room, after telling her their affair was over; his wife was coming home from abroad as a contract worker. The bobo awoke, yelling in pain, feeling very much diminished. The woman, a modista, always had a pair of scissors in her bag. Case dismissed by Judge Aurora Reciña. The Tsikboy simply got tired of appearing in court with a towel wrapped around his head and hearing, "iyan ang naputulan." We invoked denial of a speedy trial. His manhood had become Exh. E, in a bottle.

As I understand it, in the U.S.. Congress may not detain anyone, unless it first secures an arrest order from a court when the resource person refuses to talk, invoking the 5th, even after assurance of immunity. Courts routinely cooperate. A test case may be needed here lest Faeldon be detained until the cows come home.

Last week the cows came home for Tony Cortes, my law classmate, who will miss our emerald anniv program tomorrow in San Beda. The friends of one's youth are the finest one can ever have, to paraphrase Robert Penn Warren in All The King's Men. Tony was a good lawyer who was with nationalist Abe Sarmiento, for decades, before the latter joined the Supreme Court.

Last Sunday, I attended the Sto. Niño march-procession in Mendiola; for the first time ever, I couldn't complete it. We're ageing and ailing and current events can only aggravate our condition. Such as Rappler's fate. Its true unforgivable crime is being critical of the Prez. Had it been brown-nosing Digong, Maria Ressa, like blogger Mocha Uson, might have even been invited to accompany him on his trips abroad. Thus, a conundrum.

When you reach a fork in the road, take it, NY Yankee Yogi Berra's sage advice I am reminded of cuz of the weird insistence that PNoy be charged with reckless imprudence resulting in homicide for Mamasapano; the latter offense does not involve malice or moral turpitude. I became a widower cuz of reckless driving, upping my familiarity with it.

A reckless imprudence accused is entitled to probation on conviction, for "mere" recklessness, no matter how painful the consequence is to the victim or his survivors. PNoy's legal team is quiet and should not protest too much. Or at all.

But, graft, filed by gutsy Ombudsman Chit Morales, is something else. One charged with it, as PNoy is, in effect is being labelled a crook. No probation necessarily available on conviction for a grafter. Bad faith is involved. Evil and malice mark the offense.

The Mamasapano operation resulted in terrorist Marwan being sent to the Muslim paradise where virgins await deflowering by a martyr. Casualties? One should remain a civilian or avoid being sent to fight historically fierce Muslim warriors to avoid the risks that go with joining special operation forces against them. Lore has it that Black Jack Pershing had the lethal .45 pistol devised to stop fanatical Muslim juramentados. Howling dervishes, sort of.

And it should be Mamasapano 62 to include the Muslim victims. Their lives also mattered. Not to forget that the goal of bagging Marwan by those singing "ang mamatay nang dahil sa 'yo" was attained. So, not a total failure unlike Jack Kennedy' s Bay of Pigs and Bill Clinton' s Blackhawk Down debacles. Neither was charged for failure. And rightly so. They answered to their conscience, and to history. "La historia me absolvera," cried Fidel Castro. "History will absolve me." They were not asked to pay the families of heroes or victims of collateral damage for judgment calls in good faith. If there is financial assistance, well and good, but heroism is not necessarily monetized.

The Constitution cannot and does not require a Prez to be perfect or infallible. To err is human. And here, PNoy was not in noncompliance with any statute in our scofflaw nation. Washington enlisted the aid of chemist Sean Connery, a convict, in the movie, The Rock. In the film Dirty Dozen, the convicted murderous maniacs (e.g., Charles Bronson, death by hanging, Digong's weapon of choice, as it were) became heroes. And former Top Cop Alan Purisima is only an accused, charged with PNoy. Not even a convict.

Charged reportedly with violating Sec. 7 of R.A. No. 3019 (1960) and Sec. 8 of R.A. No. 6713 (1989), is Chief Justice Meilou Sereno; everyone in government from Prez Digong down to the last barangay dogcatcher may have a problem. Said Sec. 7 mandates filing by a public servant, of "a statement of the amounts and sources of his income, the amounts of his personal and family expenses and the amount of income taxes paid for the next preceding calendar year." Its Sec. 2(b) defines a"public officer" as including "elective and appointive officials and employees, permanent or temporary, whether in the classified or unclassified or exemption service receiving compensation, even nominal, from the government. . . ."

If the House, busy with impeachment, looks at compliance with Sec. 7, its members should be prepared to show their own filings thereunder. If the Prez or his Cabinet members, or any one else for that matter, can show compliance with Sec. 7 last year, I'll eat it.

This provision may cover the fascinating consultative body the Prez created last week. Misogynistic, I submit, for naming only one woman out of 19 (thus far). From where I sit, she may be a household word only in her own household, with all due respect. Ka Celing Muñoz-Palma she isn't; no wonder she is named Ms. Susan-Hubalde Ordinario, maybe to stress that Digong much cares for ordinary folk. There are six more vacancies so there is time to heed the saying that the best man for the job is a woman, to join Ms. Susan, who I wish Godspeed (the name of co-star Nicholas Cage, in The Rock).

The body of consultants will meet for a year, derailing and shooting down Speaker Bebot's reported choo-choo bullet train arrival date of May 2018. Its members must be preparing now to comply with Sec. 7 of R.A. No. 3019 which requires one to file the required statement within a month "after assuming office." We need to know where its office will be, whether the members can hire staff, etc.. Indeed, paging DBM Sec. Ben Diokno: how much will the consultancy cost the taxpayer? I bet he cannot find a single tree with money growing on it. The Constitutional Consultants, comprising an ad hoc body, will work for about a year.

Our present Consti has a State Policy against dynasties. Yet, we saw a Prez Duterte, Mayor Duterte and Vice Mayor Duterte. I seem to be the only one to grouse about it. Maybe others do but of which I am not aware. All seem to be afraid of the Godfather (I pretend not to be). The foreign model we now have seems to have originated in Sicily.

Basically, the problem has been one of implementation of our laws. A scofflaw nation we have been since Macoy - Digong's idol - took over in the 60's and opened his William Saunders' account in Switzerland while Imelda opened her Jane Ryan's. Money for The Restoration?

Will a new Constitution make a difference?

Yup, Rappler' s mortal sin is that it has not behaved like Mocha Uson, who venerates the Godfather, who commends Aung San Suu Kyi on Rohingya, urging her to ignore us, useless human rights critics and advocates.

I have ageing-ailing issues. And I don't know what type of federalism we may get into. What I now seem to see arguably can be traced to Sicily, with a fellow Bedan for a Godfather (Duterte), capo di tutti capi, boss of all bosses, aided and abetted by Bedan Consigliere (Medialdea and Aguirre). And enforcers like Bato de la Rosa implementing a population reduction program. Another Bedan is gutsy Leila de Lima, our own Dolores Ibarruri, La Pasionaria.

At this point lawyers, led by the IBP, I for Inspiring - OK, Integrated Bar of the Philippines) , cannot do more than warn fervently against a Balkanizing federalism which may lead us to become Somalia or Venezuela, basket cases. At some point, lawyers may file cases but per se any chacha effort cannot be enjoined. More speech, not less. The noises and sounds of democracy.

Gising! Bangon! Manindigan! Shakespeare wrote, "first thing we do, let's kill all the lawyers," in praise, not dispraise, of the profession. They ask the foolish questions of the day, as Tañada, Diokno, Salonga, Arroyo, et al. did, when Digong's idol ruled and reigned and ruined our values, processes and institutions from which we have yet to recover. If we ever will, . . . enslaved as we have been for centuries.

"When will [we] ever learn? Long time passing. . . ."

The Catholic Bishops, who have played key roles in changes in the past, have warned against a "creeping dictatorship, " which some see even now as "galloping. "

I am more concerned about "political syndicalism, " as it were.

--

Saguisag & Associates Lawyers 4045 Bigasan Street, Palanan1235 Makati Office Nos. (+632) 551-6350 /833-4140 Fax No. (+632) 831-2276.

ooooo

6

Confucius and the Inevitability of Rape

Rene Saguisag
Dateline, Feb 7, 2018
Manila Times Opinion Columns

If rape is inevitable, lie back and enjoy it." When my long-time and valued friend, Foreign Affairs Secretary Raul Manglapus, said it, he got thrashed-talk all over the place. In fact, I had heard it often before, from various sources. Indeed, my ultimate source is Confucius (born 551 B.C.?), from China, a country of very smart and shrewd people.

Napoleon was right, when the sleeping giant (China) awoke, the world would tremble. We are trembling now, aren't we? Or "lying supinely on our backs" - in the words of Patrick Henry in his 1775 "give me liberty or give me death!" speech (Prof. Ipe Dino made us memorize and recite it as freshmen in San Beda).

China has effectively and subtly taken over the disputed isles in the West Philippine Sea. The administration falls all over itself in rationalizing and speaking for China, which cleverly lets its local arguably caponized spokesmen do all the work. The new twist is Presidential Spokesperson Harry Roque now plays the Blame Game and thrashes PNoy, who has been out of power for 20 months. Assuming softie PNoy were to account, when rape first was first attempted, he resisted by going to an arbitral tribunal (where my pal, Paul Reichler, who attended Harvard and trained in Arnold & Porter, as I had done earlier - won. He had also beaten in the World Court his own native U.S.A., for Nicaragua, which ruling the former ignored until there was a regime change years later, when Violeta Chamorro took over. I am verifying whether some settlement was reached. Paul and I had worked together, in another matter, for our government).

What have toughies Digong and Harry done? Jetski? Lie back and enjoy being deflowered? Or as fair Laetitia did, prevent being raped by Fireblood by giving her timely consent? Again and again, the new regime has consented. *Alalaong baga kung saan nadapa duon tumihaya?*

PNoy and Digong have Chinese blood. And so does Cardinal Tagle. And so did Cardinal Sin and Rizal. And how many of us can really say we do not have a smidgen of it? Are we ripe and ready to be super-bully China's 24th province? Digong and his advisers had better reassure us that it ain't so in the same manner that we are leery of being America' s last plantation. But, the administration dissembles, not only as to China.

Digong mow says he is for a "hybrid" form of government, whatever that means. A hybrid government for a mongrelized nation? Askals? Asong Kalye. But every dog, it is said, has its day. Will we?

Last Saturday, it was Lions day, and night, in Mendiola as Bedans came home, from all over. When I came in early that evening, certain senior alums on stage belted out the rousing sing-able The Red and The White, the origin of which I have not been able to trace and which has since been discarded in the NCAA, sadly.

At 78, last August, I, a Leo, seemed to have been the oldest alum among those who attended the Mendiola reunion, now in our Second Adolescence. OK, older was Fr. Benildus Maramba, OSB - which we used to say stood for Order of Society Boys, party animals; he is my first cousin-in-law, who quickly gave me another Rosario on first contact. Other alums may have left early when the night was still young, mayhap to be with their lovely Rosarios elsewhere.

This week, our paper carried pages from the past on the drug (opium) problem in the Philippines in the 1930's when our Guv-Gen was Chester Davis (the famed and coveted Davis Cup in tennis was named after him). At this time, we note how ancient the drug problem is and there are reports on how vicious Fentanyl could be. Prez Digong acknowledges using it as a pain-killer. It is also a people-killer. See "Fentanyl kills 16 in English city," Phil. Star, Feb. 5, 2018, p. 15, col. 5. So careful, Mr. Prez, we wish you well and pray that you change in some ways, and succeed, "for our good and the good of all His church [our people]".

The Manila Times of February 3, 1930, p.1 (page or blast from the past), as reprinted here last Saturday, recounted that a League of Nations Opium Mission arrived that morning, to "interfere," what else? The body was composed of two Swedes, a Belgian, a Czech and a Brit. The party was met on board by a PC Colonel, who did not denounce the interference, and in fact brought the party to Malacañang. Today, Digong and Bato de la Rosa would tell a similar mission where to go. Not to China, where shabu (worth billions) apparently continues to come, through our porous shorelines.

Guv-Gen Davis placed at the visitors' disposal the government's facilities for assistance. It had been formed at the instance of the British government and its ultimate purpose was to help devise legislation to lessen the evils of drug trafficking. The commission had visited ten places and would visit five more and thence to Geneva about the middle of April 1930. That night, Davis gave a Palace banquet in honor of the commission dealing with a long-time problem. Ambeth Ocampo wrote in the Inquirer in April 2016 that Rizal tried Mary Jane (marijuana).

As I also said here in 2016, Tibo Mijares wrote in the Conjugal Dictatorship: "[Y.S.] Kwong made the stunning revelation that Josefa Edralin [Macoy's Ma] was arrested in Arellano High School for having opium and heroin in her possession. Kwong even mentioned the name of the arresting officer as Telesforo Tenorio, then a detective but later . . . a chief of police of Manila. The suspicion was that Josefa was selling drugs to the students of the school where she was a teacher and librarian. According to Kwong, Josefa was able to either bribe or cry her way of out the incident." Page 257.

Speaking of American Guv-Gens, we also should recall at this time of year Frank Murphy, as we mark Manila's liberation in February 1945. After him was named what is now known as Camp Aguinaldo. Murphy was the last U.S. Guv-Gen here, the last one, as a Justice, I would have thought would take the side of Yamashita when his case reached the U.S. Supreme Court. I emotionally and heatedly blasted Yamashita in our class in Harvard Law in 1967-68, to my classmate' resounding approval - they applauded; it took me decades to realize the wisdom of not succumbing to the high feelings of the moment for in the sober afterglow we may realize the sorry implications of emotionalized Fire! Aim! Ready! crusades. This I seem to see in the current Dengxavia controversy. Clint Eastwood's sage advice is for one to know his limitations. Medical expertise is not universal, on autopsies, a distinct specialty.

Last Tuesday, I saw here a pix of Mayor Erap Estrada and Veep Leni Robredo marking the Liberation of Manila, a bloody month-long (Feb. 3 to Mar. 3, 1945) episode in which 100,000 were killed south of the Pasig. Admiral Sanji Iwabuchi (when defeat was imminent, he committed suicide, said in Japan to be the sincerest form of apology; unknown here, masakit yata) was in command of 12,000 Marines. But, it was Tomoyuki Yamashita, who had lost communication and control over his 4,000 soldiers, who was executed; he was up north in the bloody month-long battle. It gave rise to the controversial Yamashita Standard of command responsibility. That may also be the Nuremberg Standard, thanks to Hitler.

But getting more and more widespread is the use of the Hitler-Duterte salute, with fists thrust forward. This was standard and expected of Hitler's storm troopers, the reason Aussie Spymaster Nick Warner got pummelled and pilloried from pillar to post for doing the fist bump with Digong. Our own people are either too scared or too ignorant not to to be lemmings. Fellow Bedans are ignorant?

Anyway, a son told me last Tuesday San Beda is now a university.(?) When I entered San Beda, in 1955, a promdi from Pasig, it was but a small college, but like Daniel Webster, speaking of Dartmouth, I say, there were those of us who loved it, and always will.

There I learned much about fierce Muslim warriors who never submitted to Imperial Manila; this may be an argument whhy there is martial law in Mindanao, and always will, or should, according to the Supreme Court, if I read correctly its latest excrescence, from where I sit, as a fervent student of human rights.

--

Saguisag & Associates Lawyers 4045 Bigasan Street, Palanan 1235 Makati Office Nos. (+632) 551-6350/833-4140 Fax No. (+632) 831 2276.

ooooo

7
"Mon Ami, You've to Start Somewhere"

Rene Saguisag
Dateline, Feb. 28, 2018
Manila Times Opinion, WFA Yahoogp

The February 10, 2018 issue of the Daily Inquirer bannered: "DU3T to Int'l Court: Why start with me? President Duterte questions the ICC [Int'l Criminal Court] decision to start its preliminary examination of alleged crimes against humanity in Asia with him when `massacres&# 39; are occurring in many other countries in the region."

Why do Frenchmen kiss a woman's hand? In 1986, in a breakfast meeting we had in Manila Hotel with Secretary of State George Shultz, he recounted this answer of a Frenchman: "Mon ami, you have to start somewhere."

The defense of selective prosecution, unequal protection or invidious discrimination will only work, if shown that "justice" is maladministered with an evil eye and an unequal hand.

But for Digong, there's always the risk of winning of course, by mounting a credible vigorous defense.

It is no defense "though"" that so many robberies are occurring anyway so why single out suspect John Doe? And here, there may be other damaging facts.

Only last August, 32 were killed in one day, in Bulacan, in the anti-poor war against drugs. An ecstatic Malacañang, perhaps concerned over our population explosion situation, said Kill-Pa-More. Digong is the only one in the region bragging about his population production program, which no one has copied in dealing with a drug problem going back beyond a century [not only during PNoy's watch, believe you me].

Digong's idol, Marcos, would deny, deny, deny. Or at least, dissemble. Macoy knew that fish is caught by its mouth but he lost anyway in Switzerland, Honolulu and Seattle. Billions were returned as ill-gotten wealth after the July 15, 2003 decision of the Supreme Court, which inexplicably did not order the prosecution of the "ill-gotteners ". The Marcoses are now where they are, working furiously for their Restoration, emboldened by Macoy's transfer to the LMB (damaged and downgraded in my view to Libingan ng mga Mandarambong at Berdugo).

As PNP head Bato de la Rosa, equally very talkative, said, his men now would he "more responsible" , after being pulled out from the back burner. Was the abandoned original Tokhang "responsible" at all? Why the pull-out "then" (which could also harm Digong in the ICC)?

To me, unlamented by the Church and the human rights community, and perceived as "irresponsible ," bloody and messy, the failed policy indicates why it was abandoned, reacting to local and global outrage. The PNP (Pulis Na Patolas) was told to back off. Too many of the poorest of the poor had died. Now the ICC has taken notice, and not improperly, from where I sit.

A state-sanctioned crime against the poor is not a crime against humanity?

The revised PNP program is an admission that the bloody messy program of dealing with a century-old problem, which no country has aped, had been a colossal failure, resulting in the death of the poorest of the many who are poor. Now, I shift to a friend who is not poor but whose heart is very much in the right place.

Again flavor of the week is my very dear friend, Loida Nicolas-Lewis, a "pal" of my youth. Last Monday we had lunch in Vicky Garchitorena's place. Tatti Licuanan, Lirio Covey, Yoly Fenix, Bert Fenix, Sonia Malasarte-Roco, and Ditas Rivera-da Silva attended. (The next night, Solaire, some re-assembled, to dancexercise in the hotel's Eclipse.)

Our thoughts were with Loida, who is unwelcome in Davao City. *Personae non gratae*, along with Sen. Sonny Trillanes. Why? Knowing her, she fights intensely for what is right and prevails by the force of reason, not by reason of force. EJKs don't amuse her.

Presidents have to thrive in a hardy climate, "and" not be *balat sibuyas*.

Loida has been a friend since college days. Then it turned out that Reggie Lewis, her would-be husband, and I, were in the Harvard Law graduating class in 1968. In 1998, Loida funded my travelling and joining our 30th anniversary reunion (full disclosure). I am incredulous at what Digong and Davaoenos have thought and done to her, and Senator Sonny. Yup, *personae non gratae*. No fair.

We should have room not only for brown-nosing Mocha Usons but also for those whose thoughts we may disagree with, and indeed even despise, in a robust democracy. More democratic space, not less.

In 1967, "my only" sister finished in UP (two engineering degrees) and I attended the graduation rites in Diliman. Among the graduands were best friends Loida and Violy Calvo (gone, the first wife of Senator Frank Drilon).

Former serious Student Catholic Action stalwarts would not go out of the law to oppose. Loida credibly denies Digong's charge that she was behind the ICC case against Digong.

I have reason to believe that all of us now into our second adolescence are respectful of human rights and against extrajudicial killing. Maybe even judicial killing. Or even killing one, softly.

SSS chief Dean Amado Valdez and Commissioner Pompee La Viña deserved better than being killed softly, fired unceremoniously.

Infighting? I see nothing wrong with creative tension in itself. But, the way Digong arrogantly mishandles dismissals is sad, leading to misperception.

He has to try to be kinder and gentler. A little ceremony recognizing the two for having done their tasks well would have been better. Tatti Licuanan's departure could also have been done in a better way. Too many foreign trips? It looks to me she has justified each one..

Tourism Secretary Wanda Teo may justify her many foreign trips but, with a make-up artist (per the Star)? However, with a courageous and influential brother in Mon Tulfo, she won't get the Tatti treatment.

While the other day was special(Ash Wednesday and Valentine), I'd prefer to cite

Digong's repetition of the demand to return the Bells of Balangiga. But now, two U.S. Congressmen object unless there is some improvement in the situation posed by the bloody, messy anti-poor war against drugs.

What can I say? Digong, Bato, you have to start somewhere. At Mass the other evening in spacious San Isidro in Pasay, I saw emblazoned HUWAG KANG PAPATAY. An apt writing on the wall. Nice to have a sweet comic funny Valentine but not to forget that dust we all are, and to dust we all shall return.

Saguisag & Associates Lawyers 4045 Bigasan Street, Palanan 1235 Makati Office Nos. (+632) 551-6350 <+63%202% 20551%206350/833-4140 Fax No. (+632) 831-2276 <+63%202% 20831%202276

oooooo

8

Is God necessary?
by Hilarion M. Henares Jr.,
July 14, 2018, The Day of the Bastille

Comes now Doctor of Psychology Steven Pinker of Harvard, whose 8 books elicited praise from Bill Gates ("most inspiring I ever read") and from London Times, New York Times and Time magazine ("sweeping, erudite, sharply argued, fun to read, highly persuasive"), asking: Is God really necessary? Do we need God to tell us what is right or wrong, what is good or bad, in other words, to establish a code of morals that allow us to live with each other in peace as befits human society? Not so, says Pinter, morality arises from a human need and is established in the Golden Rule, "Do unto others as you would like others to do unto you." From the beginning of time, in all ancient civilizations with their pantheons of capricious deities, long before Judaism, Christianity and Islam ever existed, this precept was the basis upon which human society flourished. The concept of God came into being only because men were confused by forces of nature beyond their control and understanding, and needed to have an Almighty God to attribute these forces to. Eventually this God assumed responsibility for our code of morals as well.

Morality then became part of Religion, and consisted in obeying the dictates of God, and enforced by reward and punishment in this world and the next after-life. This "add-on" becomes necessary because in this world, no moral guardian can possibly detect and punish every wrong-doing, so we have to invent a God who, like Santa Claus, is always there – "he sees you when you're sleeping, he sees you when you're awake, he knows if you've been bad or good, so be good for goodness' sake." Otherwise, God will smite you down and damn you to hell and eternal fire.

This theistic morality, according to Pinter, has two basic flaws: (1) there is no good reason to believe that God exists, and (2) there is most certainly no God to dictate and enforce moral precepts.

First, there is no God because Science and Reason cannot prove that he exists, and because the reasons given for his existence – faith, revelation, scripture, tradition – cannot be trusted to explain why different religions declare mutually incompatible beliefs on how the human race was created, on how their devotees are to behave. Scientific absurdities like Genesis have been refuted by Edwin Hubble with the Big Bang Theory; the story of Adam and Eve has been refuted by Darwin's Origin of the Species.

Second, there is no God to dictate and enforce, as Sextus Empericus in ancient times posited: "Is God willing to prevent evil, but not able? Then he isn't omnipotent. Is he able, but not willing? Then he is malevolent. Is he both able and willing? Then why doesn't he abolish evil?" David Hume puts it another way: Either God is not benevolent or he is not omnipotent; either way and in both ways, he is incapable of being God.

On the other hand, a few years ago, I wrote that there are 6 arguments used to prove there is a God: (1) Ontological (God exists because nothing greater than God can be conceived); (2) Cosmological (Everything has a cause except God who is the First Cause); (3) Argument of Miracles (Miracles happen, and only God can make it happen); (4) Argument from Religious Experience (Personal visions are direct encounters with God), (5) Argument of Utility (Belief in God is a great and indispensable moral influence), but the one argument with the widest appeal is (6) Teleological, or Argument of Grand Design, as I wrote it then, as follows:

Prior to the 20th century, most scientists believed that our universe never had a beginning, that mass, space, time and energy had always existed. Then in 1928 Edwin Hubble discovered that the universe is expanding, and using and reversing its velocity and direction, scientists calculated that the universe was born 13.8 billion years ago, from one explosion called the Big Bang, at a single time from a single pinpoint, from nothing, just like it says in the Bible, Genesis 1:1. The scientists have struggled so long up the mountain of knowledge, only to find that Bible scholars were already there at the top, long before they arrived.

If the rate of expansion of the Big Bang were a fraction less, the universe would have re-collapsed even before it reached its present size; if it were a fraction more, stars and galaxies could not have been formed, and we wouldn't be here. Conditions for life to exist (the existence and distribution of elements; the size, temperature, relative proximity of stars and planets) need to be just right that the chance against it to happen from a chance explosion of the Big Bang, defies the laws of probability – calculated to be one chance against a trillion repeated 12 times, or 10 to the 144th power, or 1 followed by 144 zeroes -- equivalent to the chance of a blind person finding one specific grain of sand from all the beaches in the world, or one person winning a mega-dollar lotto, a thousand consecutive times, with the same set of numbers. The only logical conclusion is that life came into being by deliberate design of a Superior Intellect, like the Bible says.

Then in 1953 Watson and Crick discovered the DNA in every cell of every living thing, a mere pinhead, each of which contains information equivalent to a stack of paperback books that would encircle the earth 5,000 times – an extremely complex software that reveals such intelligence that it staggers the imagination. Can it be that Science finally discovered God?

Now I remember, when I was in 4th year high school in Ateneo de Manila, being told that the first thing we do to understand the universe, the world we live in and man's role in it, is to understand the concept of entropy or disorder. In Physics it is expressed in the Second Law of Thermodynamics, which is that "in an isolated system, entropy never decreases." Confused? So was I! I asked my physics professor please to define entropy in terms I can understand, and he answered, after few unsuccessful attempts, "Well, a cup of coffee cools down, ice melts, fire warms you up, damn it, I cannot do better than that. My own professor in the University of the Philippines, could not make me understand, so forget the definition. Entropy is all around us, that is all I can say!" I was 14 years old then.

I was 20 years old in Boston, when I asked my professor in the Massachusetts Institute of Technology the same question, and he answered, "That question, Henares, is equivalent to asking me if I read Shakespeare, and my answer is that I read Shakespeare, but I cannot quote all of what he wrote." This is what Steven Pinter does in his new book "Enlightenment Now" devoting parts of several chapters to entropy, too long and too obtuse, and perhaps too erudite, to make sense to an old fogy, an engineer like me, who wants to explain a scientific law in a few paragraphs, or in one mathematical equation, like F=ma, or E=mc squared.

The dictionary does not help either. It defines Entropy as "a theoretical value measuring a property of a substance, as steam, under given conditions, upon which depends the amount of heat energy not transferable to mechanical work."

Today at the age of 94, with an IQ of 170, after having read 25,500 books in my lifetime, all of a sudden, this minute, this second, in a flash of divine inspiration, I woke up from a dreamless sleep, opened my eyes and at last, I begin to understand. So let me share my thoughts with you.

Entropy is a state of disorder, a state of being "disorderly and useless." Nature strives for disorder and uselessness, because the laws of probability dictate that there are infinitely more ways of being disorderly and useless, than being orderly and useful. It takes an artist an hour to build a sand castle, but it takes only a wave, the wind, a sea gull, and a small child to destroy it in seconds. It takes a jackass a minute to kick a barn down, an accidental fire to destroy it, or a tornado, an earthquake, a typhoon, a stick of dynamite and a hundred ways to blow it away in a few minutes --- but it takes a carpenter a whole week to build it.

13.8 billion years ago, in a split second, an incredibly dense atom exploded in a Big Bang. Suddenly, there was zero entropy, all was a flash of energy so useful and orderly that it gave birth to our Universe. Entropy increases as this incredible energy is wasted in moving galaxies away from each other. While stars are born, burn out and die, while black holes proliferate and suck into nothingness all matter within reach – entropy increases, till at last at the end of time and existence, the cold stars and dead planets are dispersed sparsely into the universe, a thin soup like salt in the ocean, useless and disorderly.

In my dissertation on the existence of God, I was wrong to assume that the universe is in a state of perpetual balance, and that this state is the result of a Grand Design of a superior intellect that we can do no better than to call God.

That instance of improbability measuring one chance against "one followed by 144 zeroes," is precisely the infinitely small sliver of a chance that life could exist in only one planet among 12 planets in our solar system, among a billion stars in our galaxy, among a hundred billion galaxies in the universe. The Second Law of Thermodynamics is at work against a vast and irresistible tide of entropy, the First Law of existence, expressed also in Murphy's Law (what can go wrong, will go wrong); Forest Gump's "Shit Happens"; Things fall apart; Rust never sleeps. Thus the Law of Entropy allow for only a hopeless past and a depressing future. Yet we stand in awe and in wonder of it all! ---

Because from one vantage point The Law of Entropy defines the fate of the universe and the ultimate purpose of life, mind and human striving – and that is, to use an infinitely small part of that energy -- to plant a tree, to sire a son, to write a book, to employ our knowledge and reasoning to the hundred million things that we do to build our civilizations, and to achieve our final destiny.

Because, according to the same Law of Entropy, randomly and unexpectedly, after 13.8 billion long long years, atoms arrange themselves to carve out infinitely minute oases of beneficial order and usefulness, to give us sunsets, rainbows, clouds, snowflakes, a stolen kiss. an orgasm, flora, fauna, the very existence of Man, and the most inspiring concept of God! #

Ooooo

9

Is the Human Race necessary?

by Larry Henares
August 6, 2018

In a previous article I ask if God is necessary, and quoted Steven Pinter who said that God does not exist, nor is he necessary. And he goes on to say that all that is necessary is Reason, Science and Humanism, and the revitalization of all the human values derived from Age of Enlightenment that originated from the Western World: Life and the Pursuit of Happiness; Liberty, Equality, Fraternity; Democracy, Free Will, Free Market Economy, Individualism, Self Determination, Liberalism. And counter to the Enlightenment are obviously (1) Religious Faith and (2) the Tribalism of clans, tribes, ethnic groups, religion, race, class and nation-states. It seems that Steven Pinker is afflicted with that demonic of all idolatries -- arrogant Self-Worship, of the white race and the Western Man -- that leads ultimately to self-destruction, which we will prove later. It is our honest opinion that Pinker is indulging in intellectual masturbation.

First let me answer the first question posed: Is God necessary? I may for the sake of argument, concede that it is irrelevant whether or not we believe in the existence of God. But I do believe that whether he exists or not, God is necessary. If one did not believe that there is just and merciful God, and that immortal souls will meet again after death, life on earth would be intolerable. It would have no purpose, no everlasting love, no ultimate justice. Life would not be worth living. But we do believe, and hope and pray that someday in God's own time, we will be reunited with our beloved ones departed, my father, mother, my father- and mother-in-law, my brother, my sister, my sisters-in-law, my adopted brother, many friends, and my ever loving wife Cecilia. It is this hope of reunion for all eternity that sustains us in our hour of loss and bereavement.

Endless are the ways that man worships, ranging from the horrible to the sublime to the ridiculous -- proof that whatever else he may be, Man is a religious being -- the only creature, according anthropologist William Howells, "who comprehends things he cannot see and believes in things he cannot comprehend."

Most living religions assume that they come directly from the hand of God, unique like the biblical Melchisedec, "without father, without mother, without descent, having neither beginning of days, nor end of life." But that is not so. The Dead Sea Scrolls show that some ideas and rites of the New Testament are similar to those of the Qumran sect that existed a century before Christ. The 4,000-year-old Babylonian epic of Gilamesh finds striking parallels in the Genesis story of Noah's ark.

And how can faiths which hold salvation to be a reward of man's own striving, merge with faiths that insist salvation is an unmerited gift of God? Or the Eastern belief that truth is found at the end of a human quest, reconcile with Western faiths that truth is revealed by an act of Revelation? How to synthesize the Christian conviction that Divine Revelation culminated with Jesus, with the Muslim conviction that a more complete revelation came with Mohammed, and the Jewish belief that neither surpassed the Law and the Prophets?

Many non-believers like Pinter, turn to the philosophy of Humanism which holds the view that men have but one life to lead and should make the most of it in terms of creative work and happiness, but that is also a faith, faith in Homo Deus. Communism which regards religion as the opium of the people, is fast developing into a church. If as the New Testament says, faith is "the substance of things hoped for, the evidence of things unseen," then Communism, with its promise of a classless social order and equal sharing of all men in the benefits of life, surely is a faith. It may be that God is imbedded in the human DNA.

In their religions, men do not really differ. They seek the favor of their gods, protection from danger, community with their fellows, courage in the hour of conflict, comfort in the hour of grief, guidance in their daily concerns, and some hope for immortality.

Today the march of science makes it imperative that Man be saved from that most demonic of all idolatries -- arrogant Self-Worship that leads ultimately to self-destruction.

Salvation comes only when, in the words of the prophet Micah, our faith inspires us "to do justly, to love mercy, and to walk humbly with God."

It is evident that Steven Pinker is trying to elevate Western Civilization and the white man, who caused so much tears and suffering to the colored races with his notions of racial superiority, to the level where we may ignore the historical grievances that have to be redressed before we proceed to pursue our Final Destiny.

Equality is unachievable. We need only to observe that handsome men tend to marry beautiful women, and that the rich and the powerful also tend to marry rich and powerful mates, and the good-looking ones too. In the long run, the human race will continue to separated into two groups, (1) the few rich, powerful and good-looking, and (2) the many poor, powerless and ugly. And not humans, but non-human persons with the human right to enter into contracts and own property, Nations and Corporations, rule the earth and own most of its resources.

Comes now Yuval Noah Harari, a Hebrew, of a race considered inferior by the Germanic races, which includes the Germans, the Dutch, the English, and the American WASPs (White Anglo-Saxon Protestant), in his book, Homo Deus, contradicting everything that Steven Pinter wrote about the Final Destiny of the Human Race.

Recent scientific discoveries, Harari writes, undermine the liberal philosophy of the Enlightenment. Liberals uphold free markets and democratic elections because they believe every human being is a uniquely valuable individual, whose free choices are the ultimate sources of authority. This belief is obsolete, and Steven Pinter is wrong, because:

First, Liberalism succeeded because in the past, political, economic, and military sense combined to ascribe value to every human being; in democratic elections because of his vote, in the Industrial Revolution because he runs the machines, in the army if he capable of firing a shot.

In the future, however, robots take over the industrial machines, sophisticated smart weapons need only a finger to push a button to conduct a war (mutually assured destruction, MAD, makes world wars unlikely) and algorithms imbedded in net-working systems take over control over the conduct of human affairs. The need for and the value of individual human beings are considerably diminished. We will all have been devalued, hahaha, like Iraqis and Afghans. Perhaps Human Beings are no longer necessary.

Second, the system will continue to find value in humans collectively in the mass (the objective is still to keep them happy and prosperous), but not in unique individuals separately.

Third, the system will continue to find value in a few unique individuals, but these will constitute a new elite of upgraded super-humans above the mass of the population.

In such a world, there is really no such thing as Free Will or Free Choice. Over the last century, bio-scientists discovered that there is neither soul, nor free will nor self – but only genes, hormones and neurons that obey the same physical and chemical laws governing the rest of reality. With state regulation, there is no real Free Markets, with monopoly by large corporations, bolstered by patents, trademarks, price-fixing, combinations and conspiracies in restraint of trade.

Actually forces are already at work in this Information Age, that tremendously increase the amount of goods available at little marginal cost, "free stuff" that are slowly undermining the Capitalistic System itself. E-mail is free, the Post Office has lost its relevance. Education is free for those who can surf the Internet. Wikipedia with its 27,000 volunteers sharing information, had driven encyclopedias out of business. Books are so cheap, easily replicated at the touch of the button, that libraries are no longer viable. The dissemination of news is free, newspapers are on the verge of extinction. Almost all the people in this planet own cellphones; that means that everybody enjoys connectivity, and land-lines and phone companies will eventually be extinct. The digital camera was invented, and Kodak was forced into bankruptcy; now everybody owns a camera, taking perfect pictures without limit without using a single sliver of silver which used to be a component of the photographic film.   With the invention of the computer, writing books and putting them in the hands of readers, is available to anyone who wants to do it. I read one book a day for 70 years of my 94 years of age, I have lived the lives and absorbed the thoughts of the authors of the 25,500 books I read, yet everything I know is available to morons at the flick of the button in the Internet. These are just a few of the many "free stuff" that are changing our lives, as the result of the convergence of digital technologies in the smart phone, the other products: clocks, maps, calendars, cameras, long playing records, tape recorders, cassette recorders, compact discs, books and magazines, even department stores.

And the miracle of it is that this Information Age is undermining the ability of the Capitalistic system itself to contrive Scarcity out of Abundance in order to generate profits. The very concept of property, patent and trademark protection is being challenged. Netizens can download practically any movie that has ever been filmed and practically every song ever composed without having to pay the people who produced them. Corporate secrets are repeatedly being hacked and leaked to the public. I believe the Capitalistic System will eventually fade away, eventually into some form of Christian Socialism that existed for centuries, in such Catholic religious orders as the Benedictines and Augustinians. The economics of caring and sharing is at hand.

The Age of Information is already preparing the world for Project Zero – because its aims are zero carbon energy system, the production of machines, products and services with zero marginal costs, and the reduction of necessary labor time as close as possible to zero.

In the Information Age of unlimited Abundance, the end purpose is to pay every one of working age, an unconditional basic income from the state, enough to guarantee freedom from want, all the things he needs to live a decent life even if he does not work. It allows everyone to volunteer, set up co-ops, edit Wikipedia, learn how to use 3D design software, or just exist; to space out periods of work, make a late entry or early exit from working life, switch easily in and out of stressful jobs. We will be a classless society of consumers who are also producers, designers, artists and lovers.

As Harari expresses it, the main products of the 21st century will not be textiles, vehicles and weapons, but bodies to a state of health, brains and minds to a higher IQ and EQ. While the Industrial Revolution created the Working Class, the Information Age will create aClass of Useless and Pampered Masses, with a guaranteed high standard of living by robots, drones and net-worked algorithms. Democracy and free market will both collapse, once Google and Facebook know us better than we know ourselves, and authority will shift from individual humans to net-worked algorithms. Humans will not fight machines but will merge with them when Artificial Intelligence surpasses human intelligence. Contrary to Sci-fi movies, we are heading towards marriage, not war.

This is the shape of the new world, and the gap between those who get on board and those left behind will be larger than the gap between industrial empires and agrarian tribes, larger even than the gap between Homo Sapiens and the Neanderthals. The way humans have treated animals is a good indicator of how upgraded humans will treat the pampered useless masses. This is the next stage of Evolution. This is Homo Deus, the Human God.

So, are ordinary, run-of-the-mill, garden-variety human beings no longer necessary? Devaluated into useless masses that exist only to be pampered and tolerated?

In 1966, in his third year high in La Salle Greenhills, my son Atom, favorite of Ninoy Aquino, decided with my help to make a movie as a substitute for a term paper, entitled "The Original Sin" the story of Mankind from Adam and Eve to the last two people on earth -- adroitly pacing the film from a farce (Genesis), to a serious documentary decrying pollution and the rape of Mother Earth, to a fantasy (the Doctrine of Divine Recall), and a human drama (James and Mary) with an O. Henry ending. The script is as follows:

In the beginning God created the heavens and the earth and everything else, and saw that they were perfect.

Then almost as an afterthought, God created Adam and Eve, and that's when the trouble began. He forbade them to partake of the Apple of His eye, the fruit of the knowledge of good and evil. But a snake in the grass enticed Eve to taste the Apple, and to get Adam to do the same. When Adam was all fired up to do what comes naturally, Eve demurred, "Close your eyes and open your lips, darling, and I'll give you a big big kiss." When he did, Eve shoved the Apple into his mouth. God was mad and ordered Adam and Eve exiled.

They went forth and multiplied.

And so the human race began. But oh such a bad beginning!

The human race began, and what a rat race!

Man multiplied so fast that he soon covered the face of the earth. Human beings scoured the ground they walked on; poisoned the air they breathed with fumes from their cars and factories. Indiscriminate use of insecticides eliminated the insects, and the birds that fed on the insects, and the plants that needed to be pollenized, till eventually came the Silent Spring --- no birds, no crickets, no plants, no flowers. They poisoned the seas and rivers with industrial waste. Chemical detergents proved indestructible by the scavengers of nature, and soon permanently contaminated the waters of the earth.

And now having raped poor Mother Earth, the human species reached out into space to ravage the rest of the Universe!

"Man has destroyed the balance of Nature and the Grand Harmony of the Universe," said Father Jake Bern (named after Joaquin Bernas, the only Jesuit in the good graces of Opus Dei), as he expounded on his Doctrine of Divine Recall in the year 2000 AD. Preaching before a small fanatic group of true believers, he proposed the final self-destruction of the human race.

"The Existence of Man is a false note in the Grand Harmony of the Universe. Man is destined for God's Kingdom in Heaven; his Earthly Existence was a mistake of Nature, an evolutionary accident that has destroyed the Balance of Nature.

"Balance, Order, and Harmony can only be restored when Man wipes himself completely from the face of the earth. God wants to recall Man from his earthly existence. Man must make the Supreme Sacrifice and get his reward in Heaven. All must come, and Now!"

And with that statement, Father Jake Bern put a pistol into his mouth and blew his own brains out.

Fifty years later in 2050 AD, the Doctrine of Divine Recall became the world religion. People began to kill themselves with hallucinatory drugs, and death became a beautiful religious experience. By 2075 AD, the World Government decreed that all women must henceforth practice birth control. Thus in that fateful year was born the last generation of the human race.

Twenty years later in 2095 AD, the babies grew old enough to understand and appreciate the Doctrine of Divine Recall. And in an unprecedented exercise of sovereign power, all the people on earth opted for the Final Solution --- the systematic self-extermination of the human race.

The mass suicide was carried out chronologically from the eldest to the youngest, till at last, the last generation of human beings --- the generation of 2075 AD --- took its turn on the rack of self-destruction. This was to be the Final Act of the Last Exodus, the glorious finale to the Fall of Man.

Bernadette was an ugly woman, a frigid misanthrope, and a fanatic true believer in the Doctrine of Divine Recall. She was chosen to be the last person on earth, entrusted with the awesome duty to oversee the death of the last batch, and kill herself.

But there were two from the last batch who plotted blasphemy. They were in love, and wanted to remain alive to produce a new human race. Their names were James and Mary.

Bernadette discovered, after the suicide of the last batch, that James and Mary had disappeared. Using a sensitive detector computer, Bernadette found them making love in a bed of wild flowers, amidst a sunset that bathed the scene with kaleidoscopic colors as far as the eyes can see, beside yawning abysmic chasms and thunderous cataracts that stagger the mind into thoughts of Time, Space, Eternity and God. This must have been how the earth looked in the beginning --- pure, pristine, virginal --- before Man came into existence.

Bernadette fired a shot into the face of Mary, and as she shuddered her final gasp, Bernadette stood there, triumphant, her pistol pointed at the last man on earth --- James.

James waited for the instant of doom. It came with a deafening roar, and momentarily stunned him.   James looked up to see the last woman on earth, smiling, her one hand stretched out with an offering of peace --- a ripe red apple. With the other hand, she discarded her pistol, and began to unbutton her dress.

And so the human race started again. But oh, another bad beginning! The End.

The proper study of mankind is Man, said Alexander Pope. Tell me the story of mankind, begged my young daughter Juno, then a sweet young lady with all the curious wisdom of her six years of age. Who can resist the challenge of one on whom the future of mankind depends? So I answered, sit still, my child, I said, and listen to this human drama, the denouement of which may yet be in your hands.

Once upon a time, thousands and thousands of years ago, a strange curious-minded creature stared through matted hair at the brilliant pin-points of light set in the velvety blackness of the night.

He asked himself "Why?" And with that question he drifted away from the beasts of the field and unconsciously started on the road to destiny.

It was a road beset by perils and pitfalls that this bewildered creature took -- this half human creature struggling to be a Man.

He was weak, but he was not helpless. His skin was bared to the elements, but he tamed fire to give him warmth and comfort. His was not the agility of the tiger nor the strength of the elephant, but he chipped the sides of a stone to fashion a weapon that gave him mastery over the animal world.

He viewed the fishes roving the deep and found that by gouging out a log into a crude canoe, he too could roam the seas. He watched birds rise in the air and wondered if he too could ever fly.

Man's progress was slow, and the sun did not always shine on his path.

Once, amidst the terror-laden blackness of the night, he stopped and realized he was terribly alone. There, in his loneliness, he found a Friend. For out of the night came a voice saying, "I am the Lord thy God..."

In a vision of another world, Man saw things more beautiful than he ever saw before. He saw pearly gates and golden streets and jeweled palaces. In seeing, he found peace and contentment and a promise of things to come.

When the vision faded, Man was filled with envious yearning. He could not wait for another world. He wanted his heaven here on earth. He would build it himself, aye, and be like... God!

Eagerly, passionately, he set himself upon his task. He took the green of the pastures, the gold of the hills, the might of the rivers, fashioned them with his hands, his heart, his mind -- and transformed them into power. He built ships that plowed the heaving oceans, planes that swept the virgin heights.

He bored tunnels through insurmountable barriers of rock. He moved mountains. He sent his merest whisper echoing throughout the world. He conquered time and space, he conquered his whole planet...

But he could not conquer himself. Evil crept into his soul and manifested itself in wars, cruelty and bloodshed. He sought peace but he brought only turmoil and confusion unto himself.

A strange restlessness grew within him. The light of knowledge served only to extend the circumference of the surrounding darkness. The more he learned, the more he realized how ignorant, how insignificant he really was, and how utterly unworthy he was of the heaven he was to build.

He who wished to be God found out that he was just a small, crawling mass of impure carbohydrate, marooned in a bit of stardust adrift in the vastness of the infinite.

Then suddenly Man made three tremendous discoveries.

First, in an infinitely minute particle of matter, he found the source of power of suns and stars.

Second, he discovered the means to free himself from the embrace of Mother Earth and reach out into the timeless space beyond.

But more exciting than nuclear power and the race to the stars, is the coming Biological Revolution. In the coiled structure of the DNA molecule and the complex arrangements of its atoms lie the final secrets of life and heredity. Once he masters its genetic code, man's powers will truly be godlike, with the ability to shape his own evolution, and create new forms of humanity.

The mystery of all creation awaits his coming.

Awestruck and confused, Man stands at the threshold of a new era. The key is in his hand. Hopeful, yet afraid, he hesitates at the door before him. What thoughts, what prayers, what visions take place within him!

Perhaps Man can now be a God. Perhaps he can now build his pearly gates and golden streets and jeweled palaces. Perhaps.

But in the light of his human failings, he wonders if he can trust himself with these awesome secrets. Perhaps, he was never meant to be a God. Perhaps the revelation of these secrets will destroy Man, will blast the world back into its elements...

...and perhaps, millions and millions of years will pass before there is a new world and a new planet... and another curious-minded creature, staring through matted hair at the brilliant pin-points of light set in the velvety blackness of the night.

Oooooo

10

My letter to grandson Larry Henares

August 1, 2018, 12 o'clock Midnight

Dearest Uno,

My favorite story about you is that when you were born prematurely, the hospital put you in an incubator beside a baby girl called Isa. It was destiny at work, I imagined, to have Uno and Isa (a couple of number Ones together with a third one called Juan or One). I was disappointed that years later, Isa grew up faster than you did, a head taller than you are, and Juan never showed up to complete the Trinity. I consoled myself with the fact that girls do grow up faster than boys do, till the age of puberty when girls stop growing and menstruate, and boys keep growing and masturbate (OMG, it rhymes!). Unfortunately, at the age when both of you start to have dirty thoughts, Isa disappeared completely out of your life, and Juan probably became Juana and eligible to be your wife (OMG, it rhymes again!). Menstruate, celibate, masturbate, ejaculate, copulate, populate, integrate, conjugate, perpetuate, soon to mate, celebrate. -- life, wife, knife, fife --- this stops right here, my dear, beer, sear, ear, fear, gear, leer, mere, near, peer, queer, tear, veer, year, we're here, -- damn it, I can't stop, sop, mop, bebop, cop, drop, fop, hop, lop, wop, pop, top..... I am going crazy, daisy, hazy, maisy, macy, tracy, stacy, racy.... Damn, damn, damn! I got writer's cramp, damp, clamp …. no no no, writer's block, sock, shock!!

Sorry, my beloved grandson Uno, I have something I never had before, a writer's block, just like St. Thomas Aquinas had, just before he died. According to G. K. Chesterton, my favorite author, master of paradox, St. Thomas Aquinas, or Tomas Aquino, no kin to Ninoy or Cory, had a beatific vision of heaven so beautiful, that everything he ever wrote paled in comparison, so he ordered his secretary to destroy all his writings which he described as "all hay", or *basura*. Fortunately, his secretary disobeyed him, but he had a terrible case of writer's block.

St. Thomas served three Popes. One day on his way to the Council of Lyon, he fell off his mule, and was taken to a nearby monastery of nuns to recuperate. As he lay on his sick bed, his writer's block disappeared, and he dictated to the nuns, his Commentary on the Song of Songs, the Canticle of Canticles, a book of poems on Human Love written by King Solomon, son of King David who slew Goliath and cut the penises of 200 Philistines to provide 200 foreskins as payment for the hand of Michal, King Saul's daughter…. and stole Bathsheba from her husband.

Solomon, you see, had 700 wives and 300 concubines, and was God's expert on *kalibogan*, on sex, on human passion, and he wrote one of the most beautiful passages in the Bible, something which I fully intended to write also for your edification. St. Thomas Aquinas' Commentary was based on a comparison between Human Love and Love of God, a theological thesis that pales in comparison to the Song of Solomon.

Thus did Tomas Aquino solve his writer's block. In the meantime, while I am nursing my own writer's block, I urge you to read G. K. Chesterton's What is Wrong with the World, or his Everlasting Man, or his Orthodoxy, or the Song of Songs by King Solomon, not in the Catholic Bible Douay, but in the more literate, the more poetic Protestant King James version, as befits my only grandchild who is a book worm, to worm your way with this *palanca*, to God on the eve of your religious retreat. Keep digging.

My everlasting love, your grandfather,

Hilarion M. Henares Jr.

ooooo

11

Rodrigo Duterte and the Original Sin

Allen Gaborro
agaborro@comcast.net
Filipino-FilAm Network,
Worldwide Filipino Alliance
July 2, 2018

Christianity has played a prominent role in Philippine history, culture, and society. On the shared understanding of the Christian faith, it has endured for some 400 years in the country with millions of Filipinos drawing spiritual strength and inspiration from its teachings.

This has translated into the willing, collective submission of Filipino Christians to Roman Catholicism as it has been imbued in their minds by centuries of religious indoctrination.

This has come at the astronomical price of surrendering critical thinking. Whenever faced with doubtful or dissenting viewpoints as regards to their beliefs, Filipino Christians have never wavered in choosing to protect the religious doctrine with little regard for logic or even common sense. But that's what faith is all about—enlightened examination or fact-finding are anathema. The faithful are expected to take the religious teachings at their word.

So when Philippine President Rodrigo Duterte bluntly included himself in the row of skeptics on the religious tale of Original Sin, the

Christian faithful came at him hard and fast and with all the indignation they could muster. This time you see, Duterte—known for his uninhibited usage of foul language and primitive insults—went too far in their eyes by calling God "stupid" and a "son of a bitch" for engendering the Adam and Eve story which in turn led to the guilt of Original Sin.

More specifically, Duterte was getting at how he surmised that Original Sin was not only preposterous, but wholly unjustified. We should be reminded that to accept Original Sin is to swallow that all of mankind is born in sin as a result of Adam and Eve's all-too human vulnerability in giving in to temptation. The story is one of Christianity's sacred and iconic narratives which easily explains the exasperated reception Duterte received for his disparaging remarks.

Atheists or agnostics like myself would dismiss the claims to veracity that Christians ascribe to the Adam and Eve story. People of our persuasion would strenuously argue that there is categorically no scientific proof whatsoever that the Adam and Eve episode ever took place. To accept it as historically true is strictly a matter of faith.

With that in mind, Duterte's criticism of Original Sin and the God that allegedly cast it upon humans cannot be passed off as a mere fancy on the president's part. The fact of the matter is that Original Sin, if we are to speak intelligently about it, is what Duterte says it is: a product of God's—if God truly exists—fatuousness and cruelty.

Duterte's loathing for Christianity's "stupid" God and Original Sin is consistent with the late atheist writer Christopher Hitchens's conviction that one of the problems of the Christian faith is that it gives rise to the disturbing idea that as human beings, "we are created sick" but that we are "commanded to be well." It's an unequivocal summation of Original Sin but also one that is accurate nevertheless. It is a summation that will offend religious sensibilities but Original Sin as it was conceived deserves to be taken to task.

Original Sin fails to live up to some of the very Christian teachings it is meant to form the basis of. The concept helped spur on the notion of existential guilt that Christians have been taught to believe they have been born with no thanks to the "rebellious" behavior of Adam and Eve.

Herein lies a huge problem with Original Sin: through absolutely no fault of our own, we come out of the womb already immersed in sin, as if we somehow committed transgressions as human cells and embryos. It is in the worst possible spirit of what can be called a preexisting condition.And we have it all because of the purported actions of two equally-purported individuals whose existence there is no historical evidence of.

The idea of being born in sin despite being inculpable in any rational way is both unconscionable and absurd. That is, if you think that God is an omnipotent, all-powerful, all-knowing force which Christians indeed think he is. Well then, the question has to be asked in regards to Original Sin: why would an almighty deity who is supposed to know literally everything that has happened and literally everything that will happen beforehand need to conduct some pitilessly, conjured up loyalty test for his first two human constructions?

I can think of three cogent explanations for this conundrum. Either the Christian God is a sadist who, akin to someone casually watching a boxing match on television, sits back and gleefully watches his creations twist and turn in pain and agony as part of their teleological mission as it has been set out for them by him. Or, the Christian God is simply not the eternally all-knowing, infinite power his followers have been led to believe. Or even more simply, God does not exist. Which is it? Is God a callously divine spectator of human failings or should we chalk it up to his insecurity and ignorance? Or has he always been a gross figment of our imagination to begin with?

Such sentiments are blasphemous to the Christian faithful because they cast doubt on either God's omniscience, his integrity, or his presence in the universe. But from a rational viewpoint, those same sentiments speak even greater volumes in that they reveal a distressing predicament embedded within Original Sin: if God created Man in his own image according to Christian teachings, then Adam and Eve's original sin is a reflection of God's own weakness and imperfection. Either that or the whole story of Original Sin is an out-and-out myth.

Let me say that the two related main points I'm ultimately making here is that one of them is unaffectedly clear-sighted. At the same time my distrust of the Original Sin story is emotionally difficult for me to assert. It came quite lucidly to me to make a stand in putting the idea of Original Sin in a deeper, more critical and judicious context. What is bothering me then is that my need to be consistently objective about all things religious has forced me to take the side of a man I personally loathe and believe to be a murderous war criminal, Rodrigo Duterte.

So yes, I do agree with the gist of Duterte's criticism on God and Original Sin. But where he went wrong was with his all-too typical bluntness which has served him well in the past. Duterte should have known better than to candidly state something that would infuriate Filipino Catholics who happen to constitute the majority of the Philippine population. Not that Filipino Catholics would have understood the president's aspersions even had he said them respectfully. But his contemptuous manner of disagreeing with the Original Sin narrative was to pour fuel on the fire of Catholic umbrage.

Duterte could have found a more civil way of expressing his views on a core value for Christians. At the very least Duterte could have shown a certain amount of modesty and humility in letting Filipino Christians know his contrarian views which he is entitled to like any other free thinking individual. But we all know by now that modesty and humility are rare phenomena in Duterte's vernacular and political discourse.

And while Filipino Christians vent their fury at Duterte for reasons of a spiritual, otherworldly nature, what those same Filipino Christians should be really more focused on is Duterte's own original sin here on earth, the original sin of promoting and facilitating the extrajudicial murder of thousands of suspected drug users and dealers around the Philippines.

Whether you agree with me or not, what should be at stake among Filipino Christians is not the moral veracity of Original Sin or whether or not there is such a supernatural state. What should be at stake for Filipino Christians is the temporal sake and social and personal well-being of their fellow beings. When thousands are unapologetically being murdered without due process, without pity or compassion, what good does believing that you are born in sin do anyone? Our priorities should lie with the world we can hear, see, smell, and touch and not in, as Prince Hamlet soliloquized, "the undiscovered country from whose bourn no traveler returns."

Oooooo

12

The ICC, Ka Pepe and Human Rights

Rene Saguisag
Apr 4, 2018
Yahoo Account

Today marks the ruby anniversary of the memorable April 6, 1978 Noise Barrage after which the April 6 Liberation Movement was named. The intrepid Movement, client of MABINI, was necessary, but not sufficient, to stop the gross human rights violations then going on.

No sovereign country strictly needs the International Criminal Court (ICC) but its poor obscure powerless inhabitants may. To withdraw from it may be another manifestation of a world in decay, a big step in the wrong direction.. During martial law, we needed Prez Jimmy Carter, Senator John Kerry, State Asec Pat Derian, et al., and Amnesty International to alleviate the plight of Marcosian human rights victims. We were more grateful than we could say for their "meddling"; in the spirit of the Universal Declaration of Human Rights our country had helped forge.

During Holy Week last, virtually no attention was given by media to the pioneer Hall-of-Famers in the Fulbright Philippines 70th Anniversary Gala Dinner - Reflections on 70 years of Excellence night, at Manila Pen. The trailblazers were Angel C. Alcala, Bienvenido L. Lumbera, Bienvenido F. Nebres, SJ, Clare R. Baltazar, Napoleon V. Abueva, Abdulmari

Asia Imao, Lucrecia R. Casilag and Conchita M. Abad, in the order their names appeared in the program. Joey Cuisia was No. 2, Cora de la Paz-Bernardo was No. 3 and I was No. 6. Thanks to Fulbright, I got to roam in the sacred precincts of Harvard Yard and in its law school in 1967-68.

During the dark years, students there got to read about the great Filipino Senator-Lawyer from Batangas, whose 31st death anniversary we marked last February 27, thusly: "It is pertinent to recall the wise words of Jose Diokno in rejecting what he termed `currently fashionable justifications for authoritarianism in Asian developing countries.&# 39; One [justification] is that Asian societies are authoritarian and paternalistic; that Asia's hungry masses are too concerned with providing their families with food, clothing, and shelter, to concern themselves with civil liberties and political freedoms; that the Asian conception of freedom differs from that of the West; that, in short, Asians are not fit for human rights.

[This] is racist nonsense . . . . Authoritarianism promotes repression not development - repression that prevents meaningful change and preserves the structures of power and privilege. . . ." H. Steiner & D. Vagst, Transnational Legal Transactions 445-46 (1986)..

The two authors were excellent team-teachers and I was lucky to have both. I am checking whether the quoted passage is carried in later editions. How we have fallen in the world's esteem since 1986. We may fall even deeper now in that too many people have died since Digong won, and he is now petulantly trying to withdraw from the ICC. Justice Claro M. Recto used the term "human rights" in 1936; that, from where I sit, was the first recorded use of the term in local jurisprudence. He is very much a part of our tradition in the great lawyer interpretation of history. In an easement case, he said: "The evidence discloses that this passage-way across the Hacienda `Begoña' is the same one frequented by carabaos . . . . Plaintiff intends not only to prohibit the defendants from using the road in question, but also from crossing the lands of the Hacienda 'Begoña,&# 39; also belonging to the plaintiff, where carabaos are allowed to roam. An act so shocking to the conscience, one is reminded, could only have been perpetrated during the feudal period when human rights were unmercifully sacrificed to property rights." North Negros Sugar Co. v. Hidalgo, 63 Phil. 664, 6.

We should arrest decay and feudalistic atavism and stay in the ICC. In another human rights area, who speaks for the young children victimized in divorce? Or those still in the womb? No one in the Cabinet, in the House nor in the Senate speaks for them. Who speaks for the commuter who will miss Uber? Judge Learned Hand counselled that "[m]any people believe that possession of unchallenged economic power deadens initiative, discourages thrift and depresses energy; that immunity from competition is a narcotic, and rivalry is a stimulant to economic progress; that the spur of constant stress is necessary to counteract an inevitable disposition to let well enough alone." United States v. Aluminum Co. of America, 148 F.2d 416, 427 (2d Cir. 1945). But Grab may grouse that monopoly was thrust upon it by market forces.

More disturbing is the sorry attempt to silence all competition and opposition, jailing Senator Leila de Lima, impeaching and Kenquoy-Warrantoing Chief Justice Meilou Sereno, ostracizing Rappler, Sonny Trillanes, et al., which could lead to a functional equivalent of a Jacksonian unanimity of the graveyard.

In the Kenquoy Warranto case, the SolGen saps CJ Meilou for not reporting income earned, expenses incurred, and taxes paid, required by Sec. 7 of R.A. No. 3019, the Tolentino anti-graft law of 1960.

May I repeat my challenge, if the Solgen can show me compliance by him, by any of his 17 assistants who signed the Kenquoy Warranto petition, or by any sitting or retired justice, I'll eat it. Certainly, it cannot be an impeachable offense, if only given the massive noncompliance with a law more honored in the breach than in the observance. Not enough jails to house all violators. All these many years, I have kept asking my studes to produce proof of compliance with Sec. 7 of R.A. No. 3019 (not Sec. 8 of R.A. No. 6713), by anyone among the million and a half in the Civil Service - in vain.

Can anyone in the supernumerary Presidential Anti-Crime Commish show his compliance with Sec. 7 of R.A. No. 3019? (And I have my doubt as to whether the Prez could create such an office, the task really of our pusillanimous meow-meow or bow-wow-wow Congress, with its obsolescent power of the purse.)

To hold the CJ liable under the SolGen's theory is to find oneself liable.

And I maintain that any Justice who has openly shown animosity to CJ Sereno cannot sit in judgment in her case, egregiously failing the Caesr's wife test in inhibition or recusation, routinely and repeatedly counselled by the Supreme Court.

"Above suspicion " is the operative term, to maintain the Rule of Law. Unaware that a quo warranto petition would be lodged, certain innocent Justices have talked too much and the only honorable course to take now is to recuse themselves, that CJ Meilou may have a sporting chance. They cannot judge their own cause. Credibility and legitimacy matter. They answer to their conscience and to history.

Let the impeachment trial go through. The sub judice rule of silence should apply to the Senators-Judges, used to mischievous play-by-play announcement long before all the evidence is in, but not to the public, in this political exercise, not litigation with its accepted limitation that no one observes hereabouts anyway. No premature ejac seen in Fire!Ready!Aim! congressional hearings.

And the Supreme Court leaks like a sieve. You wanna know what the SC will do? Subscribe to the best paper in town and read enterprising 16th Justice Jomar Canlas. Talaga pong hindi bulaang propeta. His mobility in the SC's sacred precincts is legendary.

A leaky SC inhibits and stifles free and robust discussion and the taksil leaker(s) should be the one (s) impeached. Recall the "Vision for the Philippine Judiciary" emblazoned on court walls: "A judiciary that is independent, effective and efficient, and worthy of public trust and confidence."

Saguisag   &   Associates   Lawyers 4045 Bigasan Street, Palanan 1235 Makati Office

oooooo

13

Thank you, Senator Fulbright; on being full of oneself

Rene Saguisag

Kudos! Debating was one activity I was involved in, as a stude.

Below, my Times piece last Friday, just in case you have no copy yet, the paper having come out on Good Friday.***** I hope the San Beda Law Faculty Development Program will have a resurrection. Maybe it hath not been dead, only it hath slumbered.

Thank you, Senator Fulbright; on being full of oneself

I DON'T recall ever having a column published on Good Friday, which the pious usually spend repenting. But, today, you are holding a copy of the best paper in town. A mild surprise? A culture shocker for me was my having to be in a classroom on Good Friday, in 1968, at Harvard Law. The reason I got there was that in 1967, Fr. Alex Mari Ganuza, College of Law Prefect of San Beda, instituted a Faculty Development Program, with me as the first awardee. I had not thought of foreign studies earlier, for lack of means but that program had me writing to various schools, including Harvard Law, which quickly responded with an offer of a full scholarship ($4,100, big money at the time). Still, the unaffordable cost of travel deterred me. San Beda's

P15,000 could cover it but what about the family I helped support?

The Fulbright program, on my application, came to my rescue, like a cavalry horse answering the bugle.

Last Friday evening, we had a delightful 70th anniversary celebration of its Philippine program at the Manila Pen (I have long wondered why a hotel in Makati is so called. And our contronyms: "salvage" means to save or have some pulis patola send someone to the Promised Land). I didn't have to touch the San Beda money at all but left it to cover our bunso's transfer to San Beda High from Pasig Catholic.

I think it was only this paper that had carried news of what was coming last Friday. And the other day, a columnist in another paper, wrote glowingly of his own Fulbright experience. Good news not newsworthy?

Gala dinner I arrived at the Pen a little late and was escorted to a table where awardee Cora Santos de la Paz-Bernardo was seated, next to hubby Ike Bernardo. She was salutatorian and Ike was first honorable mention in their Pasig Rizal Hi Class'56 (I was in '55). Cora hailed from Pateros, a younger sister of my classmate, Josie, also very bright and beautiful. In the table next to ours was honoree Joey V. Cuisia, with wife Vicky, both of whom would consult me on matters legal long, long ago. How time has flown.

Cora, No. 1 in the CPA exams, attended Cornell. We were two promdis privileged to go to the Ivy League. Perhaps, to the shock of some of my Section 1 classmates. Although I had finished grade school in Makati Elem in five years(accelerated) and would occasionally make the Rizal Hi honor roll, I was described in the latter's school organ graduation issue as a "galawgaw: with a boy's will to turn somersault."

The other honorees in that Fulbright Philippines 70th Anniversary Gala Dinner – Reflections on 70 years of Excellence night, were: Angel C. Alcala, Bienvenido L. Lumbera, Bienvenido F. Nebres, S. J., Clare R. Baltazar, Napoleon V. Abueva, Abdulmari Asia Imao, Lucrecia R. Kasilag and Conchita M. Abad, in the order their names appeared in the program. Joey was No. 2, Cora was No. 3 and I was No. 6. Gems of purest ray serene, a phrase I picked up as a high school junior, from Gray's haunting Elegy, which has stayed with me, giving me a sense of where I am. Thank you, Senator Fulbright. Thank you, Ambassador Kim, for a lovely way to spend a fun evening.

It was SRO. Sen Ed Angara, a man of many parts, and feats, was in the table of Ambassadors Kim and Joey. Ben Muego, a feared debater in our time, came by to say hello. So did Baby Baua, my late Dulce's Girl Friday in many a project. And many others, including one who told a daughter-in- law of mine, Judge Jackie, who texted her congrats and asked why I had not told my nuke family. It had not occurred to me to do so, a habit from time out of mind.

Rizal High reminiscences. Rizal High has also produced Jovito Salonga, Neptali Gonzales, Bobbit Sanchez, Lucio San Pedro, Botong Francisco and Pat and Wilma Tiamzon, said to head the New People's Army. The couple are out on bail, and I am a guarantor or bondsman. Cora and Ike did not mix in high school. She is from Pateros, while Ike is my fellow BatamPasig. The Pateros and Pasig Mafias engaged in a healthy rivalry. Cora married Pat de la Paz, from Colegio de San Agustin in Iloilo, who bar-reviewed in San Beda in 1963. He was No. 3 among 5,500 examinees, with 85.05 (I was only No. 6, with 84.85). He passed away in 1995, after serving in government with distinction. After more than a decade, Cora and Ike had a reunion, in matrimony.

I was a nothing HS grad but I was always in Section 1 and occasionally made the honor roll. However, our hambog barkada thought that being seen studying was disgraceful, haha. And were we bullied and insulted by teachers telling us to go home and plant camote. On rainy days we'd go to school in bakya. We were bulakbuleros who just enjoyed life in high school, and learned who Herodotus' son was, "history" being its father. We'd be ambushed by teachers who, from out of the blue, would ask us to spell "picturesque," etc.

In January 1955, Eddie Sanchez, bunso in Bobbit's brood of seven, our valedictorian, and I were playing hooky, in Quiapo. We saw extras blaring the 1-2 finish of San Beda in the 1954 bar, which I read as pointing me to that school (also, fare to and from Legarda was 15 centavos, beyond that 20). I was not to study hard until sophomore law when I was in the middle of many co-curricular commitments, in the National Union of Students and Student Catholic Action, teaching catechism at Mapa High just across, writing, debating, extempo speaking, partying, and emerging as college chess champ and member of champion softball (I was second baseman and contributed) and basketball (best seat in the house, the bench, which I warmed) intrams teams.

Pat and Wilma Tiamzon graduated with honors, who could have qualified for Fulbright, but, in their eyes, they preferred the harder right to the easier wrong (West Point prayer), loving their country with that kind of passion that whips the blood (Fred Reinfeld). They rebelled not long after the Marcoses moved to Malacañang when Macoy opened his William Saunders account, and Imelda, her Jane Ryan's, in Switzerland. Crime pays? Marcos and Duterte

Cooperation among the Swiss, the Americans and ourselves made possible the transfer of the kleptocratic loot in the billions while blood flowed, but nothing like what has flooded the streets after Digong won. A bloodbath. Given the Yamashita/Medina standard of command responsibility, Digong does not want to take part in the International Criminal Court proceeding, given the little risk of winning.

After martial law was inflicted, Marcos had his arrest, search and seizure orders (ASSOs). But, today, Digong casually orders the arrest of people like the Dimple bus owner and PUV colorum operators, arguably usurping the function of prosecutors and judges. The former conduct preliminary investigations and the latter conduct probable-cause determinations, now erased by Digong, a super-executive, super-court, super-legislature and a one-man continuing constitutional convention, doing all the work. He seems to have a messianic complex, and those who get in his way, like hief Justice Meilou, who fights for judicial independence, find themselves in a pickle.

There is a debate on what a dynasty is. I know that Prez Digong Duterte, Mayor Sara Duterte and Vice Mayor Pulong Duterte comprised a dynasty (Pulong has since resigned). Justice Potter Stewart despaired of his inability to define "obscenity" but in the end triumphantly said: "I know it when I see it." Cardinal Tagle said last Sunday: "In our world today, we have many kings, full of arrogance, lacking in humility, in our time; many of us follow kings who use violence, arms, threats, clearly showing lack of understanding and solidarity with the weak." Sino naman po kaya ang pinatatamaan? Holmes said even a dog can tell if it is being kicked or stumbled over.

Palace tutas do not see their boss as being alluded to, as the administration supposedly does not go after the innocent. And who plays god and passes judgment and discards the presumption of innocence? Some tutas may be smarter, and may acknowledge quietly that the Philippines is indeed part of "our world today." The Cardinal was talking of other places? C'mon.

May Digong this week—belated Happy Birthday, truly—do as he correctly says, piously, of Lent, not what he incorrectly does, impiously, elsewhere, at other times.

Anyway, this Sunday, Happy Easter everyone!

Saguisag & Associates Lawyers 4045 Bigasan Street, Palanan 1235 Makati Office Nos. (+632) 551-6350/833- 4140 Fax No. (+632) 831-2276

oooooo

14

SALNS In A Scofflaw Society

Rene Saguisag
Mar 21, 2018 at 10:01 PM,
YahooAccount

"Biggest Batch of Women Cadets to Greet DU30," read a headline, referring to the new women PMAyers. I made possible the entry of women into the PMA in a 1991 bicameral committee conference on Women in Nation Building - authored by my college chum, Raul S. Roco - R.A. No. 7192. (A bicam meet is conducted when the two chambers' differing versions need to be harmonized, or enhanced, making that body that powerful, as the Third House. I simply had the sex requirement deleted..

There is of course the Fourth House, the Camara de la Imprenta, where it is said a naughty lawmaker would add a zero or two at the end to a budget, say, for an Avenue, hehe.

I trust General Florencio Magsino has forgiven me by now for fathering the breach in the last bastion of machismo, to last and even > spread. Last time we met some years ago, he was still chiding me, for my impertinence.

The chauvinist Prez and the times may have not been kind to women like Senator Leila de Lima, Ombudsman Chit Carpio-Morales, journalists Maria Ressa/Pia Ranada, CHED chief Tatti Licuanan, and Chief Justice (CJ) Meilou Sereneo, for standing up to the Prez, whose expansionary appetite seems boundless. He wants total control of the government and the press. But, these gutsy undiscourageable women, like Ka Celing Muñoz Palma, doggedly soldier on.

The marathon House (of arguably namby-pamby Tutas?) hearings may finally end but then there's the remarkable and unexpected quo warranto (QW) proceeding filed by the Solicitor General, Joe Calida. All along, the talk had been of R.A. No. 6713, until Cong. Vicente Veloso (former Court of Appeals Justice) triggered a Eureka! moment in the Lower House, and in the SolGen's QW petition, Compañero Joe unexpectedly hammered on R.A. No. 3019, thusly: "80. The SALN requirement in the Charter recognized what has already been in the statute books. As early as 1960, Congress imposed that requirement in R.A. No. 3019. Section 7 of the law according states: "Section 7. Statement of assets and liabilities. Every public officer, within thirty days . . . after assuming office, and within the month of January of every other year thereafter, as well as upon the expiration of his term of office, or upon his resignation or separation from office, shall prepare and file with the office of the corresponding Department Head, or in the case of a Head of Department or chief of an independent office, with the Office of the President, or in the case of members of the Congress and the officials and employees thereof, with the Office of the Secretary of the corresponding House, a true detailed and sworn statement of assets and liabilities, including A STATEMENT OF THE AMOUNTS AND SOURCES OF HIS INCOME, THE AMOUNTS OF HIS PERSONAL AND FAMILY EXPENSES AND THE

AMOUNT OF INCOME TAXES PAID FOR THE NEXT PRECEDING CALENDAR YEAR: . . . (Caps added.)*

Interesting. If the SolGen can show me an authentic copy of a statement timely filed by him or any other incumbent where the filer disclosed THE AMOUNTS AND SOURCES OF HIS INCOME, THE AMOUNTS OF HIS PERSONAL AND FAMILY EXPENSES AND THE AMOUNT OF INCOME TAXES PAID FOR THE NEXT PRECEDING CALENDAR YEAR, I'll eat it.*

The Good Book has something to say about seeing the mote in one's eyes and missing the beam in one's own. Joe's 17 assistants who co-signed his petition may save their boss and themselves by showing us copies of their own SALNs complying with the Tolentino Law to show that we are not entirely a nation of scofflaws, or fake pretentious

Tribunes. All these years, I have challenged my studes to produce a SALN complying not only with R.A. No. 6713 (the Salonga-Saguisag Law), but also with R.A. No. 3019. Only one, a woman stude of mine, seems to have succeeded as to the latter but it was one preserved by the filer from the Dark Years; I passed her on that *fantastic * *basis alone.*

In 2012, the Civil Service Commission (CSC), the lead agency under Sec. 12 of R.A. No. 6713, tried to enforce Sec. 7 of R.A. No. 3019; the Lower (bagay talaga) House howled. The CSC was seen scampering away with its tail between its legs. Natameme. CSC, how about it, today? The law hath not been dead though it hath slept? Shakespeare's Measure for Measure.

I have always stressed that our intent in passing R.A. No. 6713 was administrative, not criminal. Thus, a vital provision is Sec. 10, on a > Review and Compliance Procedure, for correction.

Lead agency is the civil Civil Service Commission, not the punitive Ombudsman nor the Department of Justice.

What I have been suggesting is for Congress to amnesty the massive noncompliance, to benefit Presidents down to the last Barangay dogcatcher, with the caveat that thereafter, violators would be dealt with more severely, particularly lawyers.

My pal, Mon Tulfo, not a lawyer, says to qualify as a state witness, one must be "the least guilty," PDI, 3/20/18, and who therefore may know nothing or little then, so, whatever for? What Sec. 17 (e) of Rule 119 of the Rules of Court really says is the "accused does not appear to be the most guilty," but may know a lot of criminatory stuff.

On another pal Oscar Lagman's questioning in the same PDI issue the grant of bail to nonagenarian JPE, the Supreme Court, in 1946, granted bail for humanitarian reasons to Benigno Aquino, Sr., in 1947; he passed away the following year, at 47, watching a boxing match in Rizal Memorial. Uncle Jovy Salonga was released by Macoy to the custody of Auntie Lydia, a prisoner of love.

Last JPE and I shook hands in the Senate, where we were for Manang Letty Ramos-Shahani's necro, his grip was firm and he indeed looked ma-kamandag pa. Bedroom terrorist still? Indeed, how many can boast of at least 38 girlfriends, as reported in the Inquirer some years ago, if my memory is true? And counting? Frail, and deserving of release, was he, according to doctors in the Supreme Court? You're telling me. Now, he'll prosecute, vigorously.

Tough Manong JPE may be a bull-strong lead prosecutor in the trial of CJ Meilou Sereno, whom SolGen Joe Calida charged for allegedly not filing a statement under Sec. 7 of R.A. No. 3019, again, on "the amounts and sources of [her] income, the amounts of [her] personal and family expenses and the amount of income taxes paid for the next preceding calendar year." Petition, pp. 28-29. Heretofore, talk was limited to R.A. No. 6713. Now, the SolGen brought in R.A. No. 3019, and he may yet live to regret it. Again, if the feisty SolGen and his 17 assistants, all competent, who co-signed the Quo Warranto petition can show me copies of their statements mentioning said income, expenses and taxes, I'll eat them.

Not to miss the beams in one's own eyes, when pointing out the motes in others'. Such awfully sanctimonious piece of pious fiction in a country where laws are "more honored in the breach, than in the observance." Hamlet.

Anyone charged is entitled to a fair and impartial tribunal. How many Justices have prejudged the CJ and prematurely thrown their weight on the other side? Can they sit in judgment of one they have publicly condemned? It is hornbook doctrine that even if a rule be fair on its face but if it is administered with an evil eye and an unequal hand, it would violate one's basic human and constitutional right to equal protection. Yick Wo v. Hopkins, 118 U.S. 356, 373-74 (1886).

Justice must satisfy the appearance of justice? How many Justices have held their horses while evidence trickles in of some allegedly impeachable offense? whatever may be proven in regard to the Tolentino Law of 1960 and the Salonga-Saguisag Law of 1989, an impeachable offense is respectfully submitted to be out, more so if the review-and-complian ce requirement is not met.

And the unprecedented appearance in the House to make sumbong and the public statements of those who may not like the CJ, who may arguably need Dale Carnegie lessons, may come back to haunt them. They answer to their conscience and to history.

I hope to see a better Supreme Court focused on deciding cases - a lofty constitutional task - not frittering away their time in forlorn time-and energy-wasting turf struggles, dividing, and weakening the judiciary, to the delight of an irredentist presidency. But, even if so focused, decisions only seem to reflect the prevailing power situation, when and where the Palace is interested in.

That is the sin of the CJ, not kowtowing, and saying, "Yes, Master." If she had behaved like the Lower House supernumerary ooops, super-majority, she would not be impeached by the House and tried by the Senate, much less "quo-warrantiz ed", to borrow from a law classmate who floored Prof. Florenz Regalado, with his neology.

Saguisag & Associates Lawyers 4045 Bigasan Street, Palanan 1235 Makati Office Nos. (+632) 551-6350 <+63%202% 20551%206350/833-4140 Fax No. (+632) 831-2276 <+63%202% 20831%202276>

oooooo

15

EDSA's Revisionism; Fallacies
Rene Saguisag

Feb 28, 2018, Yahoo Account

The intriguing appointment of Ka Eduardo Manalo of the INC as special envoy raises serious questions on separation of church and state and whether he should also file his SALN (Statement of Assets, Liabilities, Net Worth, etc.). That was my intent in sponsoring R.A. No. 6713, the Code of Conduct and Ethical Standards, benefiting from the groundwork laid down by the UP College of Public Administration, on which principal author Uncle Jovy Salonga had relied (Uncle, again, cuz my lola and his mother were first cousins in a Pasig looban).

Sec. 3(B) of the Code defines "public officials" to include "appointive officials.... permanent or temporary, whether in the career or non-career service, . . . whether or not they receive compensation, regardless of amount." Arguable? Abangan. The Supreme Court may say my intent in the legislative arena meant nothing.

All of us who have war stories of Edsa'86, whose 32nd anniversary we just marked, have validated what the spouses Durants wrote: all autobiography is vanity.

On February 22, 1986, Juan Ponce Enrile (JPE), a genuine Edsa'86 hero, said in what sounded like a death-bed confession or dying declaration that he had cheated for Macoy by 300,000 votes in Cagayan earlier that month and that his supposed September 22, 1972 ambuscade was fake news, making skeptics give him the benefit of a lingering doubt that it was all a zarzuela to nail Cory.

To her and to us who were at Edsa beginning September 23, 1972, Edsa'86 validated that while we are grateful to JPE, FVR, Joe Almonte, Eugene Ocampo, Gringo, and the institutional parliament (Batasang Pambansa), it in fact represented the triumph of what we boycotters called the Parliament of the Streets. We were MPs (Mambabatas Panlansangan).

MABINI was among the eleven petitioners which had questioned the constitutionality of the snap polls; the Supreme Court said on December 19, 1985 that no, the show must go on, as it were (in a nation crazy about elections, whether for Prez or Binibining Palanggana).

Doy Laurel's role cannot be minimized but it was a fact that the Laurels were in bed with Macoy from 1972 to 1980, when he joined us and added sterling gravitas to our effort. Earlier businessmen Jimmy Ongpin openly, and Al Yuchengco, furtively, had joined the determined opposition redemocratization efforts.

We copied Portugal' s Carnation Revolution of April 1974, also involving colonels and civvies lasting likewise for four days with women putting carnations in the muzzle of guns, which unfortunately for the Portuguese did not have the benefit of cable television.

Has Edsa'86 failed? No overthrow of authoritarianism can be a failure, from where I sit.

Cory would openly admit that Ninoy was not the worst victim of martial law but just happened to be the most prominent. Business, which would make money even if blood was flowing in the streets (Baron Rotschild), realized that no one was safe after August 21, 1983, when Ninoy was salvaged on landing (validating Tita Aurora's "kutob ng ina", concurred in only Dr. Guy J. Pauker of a think tank - Rand); we know-it-alls dismissed the possibility in a huge meet in the home of Esto and Maur Lichauco on August 7, 1983.

Makati Business had its confetti canyons, matched in Davao by a Yellow Friday group led by the mother of Digong and therefore he could not just kick all Yellows in the teeth, out of affection and respect for his beloved mom, another genuine Edsa'86 hero. Dilawan, forever. I *am* a Yellow, and proud of it, and always will.

Anyway, Digong should really watch his language, stop bitching that his pay is not enough for his two wives (and kulasisis?) - unpresidential - and do something about the traffic situation. Not trivial at all; we are said to lose P3.5B daily cause of the traffic. But, more critical, he has also arguably violated the Constitution in an impeachable way by allowing the erection of military installations by China in the West Philippine Sea. Not enough to be dismissive about it it that anyway the missiles would not be directed at us but at America, where millions of Pinoy, not only Loida Nicolas-Lewis, have migrated. How many have, to China?

After we Malevolent/Magnific ent Twelve ended our status as America' s last plantation in 1991, "foreign military bases, troops, or facilities shall not [be] allowed in the Philippines except under a treaty concurred in by the Senate and when the Congress so requires, ratified by a majority of the votes cast by the people in a national referendum held for that purpose, and recognized as a treaty by the other contracting State." 1987 Const., Art. XVIII, Sec. 25. But, our Congress, reminiscent of what Mark Twain said, that the only distinct American criminal class is Congress, is too busy to be bothered by what is going on in the West Philippine Sea.

I credit the Star's Dik Pascual for the above insight on a seemingly impeachable offense far worse than has appeared so far in the allegations to unseat Chief Justice Meilou Sereno (not the one I endorsed in 2012 but she was chosen in a totally constitutional manner; I am appreciative of her writing finis to the case of Lenny Villa, killed on Feb. 11, 1991, which lasted 25 years, a long time for client Zos Mendoza to be anxious; also, for her joining in another well-written separate concurring opinion the ruling acquitting another former client of mine, Hubert Webb, on December 14, 2010). After what's going on, will we have the same Supreme Court, or stronger, or weaker (given Digong's transparent interest in removing someone who has crossed him)?

I wish they would simply heed the spirit of nominee Byron White's response when asked in the U.S. Senate how he envisioned his role would be as a Justice: "To decide cases."

Not to share administrative power and other distractions, given the SC's thousands of pending cases.

In January 1987, I, 47, turned down a signed Supreme Court appointment. I am a psycho with head not properly and tightly screwed on? Another proof that I was sira was that I wrote for Dik's opposition paper pre-Edsa' 86, with his wife picking up my copy Sunday afternoons.

Spousal heroes.

Digong has Chinese blood, like many of us, and he might not overly mind our becoming the 24th province of China, as he has suggested (jocosely?), but watch what he does, not what he says, haz lo que hago, no lo que digo). A referendum however may show more votes for our becoming the 51st State; I cannot imagine though why the U.S. would welcome 107M poor conejos. We do not, like Maria Clara, throw ourselves at the U.S.

If a small woman is raped by the brawny burly Barangay bully and resistance would seem futile should she not simply yield physically but resist spiritually? For this intriguing idea, the late actor Rod Navarro introed me in Pasig to the books of Donald Hamilton (Rod was a wide reader, and would not use camel when he could employ "dromedary. " We played pinball in Pasig and ballroom-dancexerci sed in Manila's Alegria and Makati's Bahia, both gone now.

Fellow Bedan Justice Sammy Martires in a remarkable intriguing ponencia says "we simply cannot be stuck to the Maria Clara stereotype of a demure and reserved Filipino woman." Hmmmmm.

You be the judge, in general. Each case though must be decided in its factual context. In Club Nautilus on Dewey (now Roxas) Blvd., also gone, it was said that the men were naughty and the girls were loose. Happy hours.

What is definitely sad in the current administration is the continuing use of the Nazi salute, illegal in some countries, topped by argumentum ad hominem, baculum et populum. Judged on language (bastos and unkind), dynasties (Dutertes, Prez, Mayor and Vice Mayor, the latter now ex-), traffic, rice shortage or hoarding, and rising prices, it has been a total failure thus far.

Can we really say corruption has been reduced and the police are more respected than dreaded?

We can all learn from Tolstoy and West Point, that good people change others, better people change the system (parliamentary/ presidential federal) but the best ones change, themselves. West Point cadets pray for them to prefer the harder right instead of the easier wrong and never to settle for a half truth when the whole can be won.

Saguisag & Associates Lawyers 4045 Bigasan Street, Palanan 1235 Makati Office Nos. (+632) 551-6350 <+6320220551206350> /833-4140 Fax No. (+632) 831-2276 <+63202 20831202276>

ooooooo

16

Confucius and the Inevitability of Rape
Rene Saguisag

Wed Feb 7, 2018, "Yahoo Account"

"If rape is inevitable, lie back and enjoy it." When my long-time and valued friend, Foreign Affairs Secretary Raul Manglapus, said it, he got thrashed-talk all over the place. In fact, I had heard it often before, from various sources. Indeed, my ultimate source is Confucius (born 551B.C.?), from China, a country of very smart and shrewd people.*

Napoleon was right, when the sleeping giant (China) awoke, the world would tremble. We are trembling now, aren't we? Or "lying supinely on our backs" - in the words of Patrick Henry in his 1775 "give me liberty or give me death!" speech (Prof. Ipe Di¤o made us memorize and recite it as freshmen in San Beda).

China has effectively and subtly taken over the disputed isles in the West Philippine Sea. The administration falls all over itself in rationalizing and speaking for China, which cleverly lets its local arguably caponized spokesmen do all the work. The new twist is Presidential Spokesperson Harry Roque now plays the Blame Game and thrashes PNoy, who has been out of power for 20 months. Assuming softie PNoy were to account, when rape first was first attempted, he resisted by going to an arbitral tribunal (where my pal, Paul Reichler, who attended Harvard and trained in Arnold & Porter, as I had done earlier - won. He had also beaten in the World Court his own native U.S.A., for Nicaragua, which ruling the former ignored until there was a regime change years later, when Violeta Chamorro took over. I am verifying whether some settlement was reached. Paul and I had worked together, in another matter, for our government).

What have toughies Digong and Harry done? Jetski? Lie back and enjoy being deflowered? Or as fair Laetitia did, prevent being raped by Fireblood by giving her timely consent? Again and again, the new regime has consented. Alalaong baga kung saan nadapa duon tumihaya?

PNoy and Digong have Chinese blood. And so does Cardinal Tagle. And so did Cardinal Sin and Rizal. And how many of us can really say we do not have a smidgen of it? Are we ripe and ready to be super-bully China's 24th province? Digong and his advisers had better reassure us that it ain't so in the same manner that we are leery of being America' s last plantation. But, the administration dissembles, not only as to China.

Digong mow says he is for a "hybrid" form of government, whatever that means. A hybrid government for a mongrelized nation? Askals? Asong Kalye. But every dog, it is said, has its day. Will we?

Last Saturday, it was Lions day, and night, in Mendiola as Bedans came home, from all over. When I came in early that evening certain senior alums on stage belted out the rousing sing-able The Red and The White, the origin of which I have not been able to trace and which has since been discarded in the NCAA, sadly.

At 78, last August, I, a Leo, seemed to have been the oldest alum among those who attended the Mendiola reunion, now in our Second Adolescence. OK, older was Fr. Benildus Maramba, OSB - which we used to say stood for Order of Society Boys, party animals; he is my first cousin-in-law, who quickly gave me another Rosario on first contact. Other alums may have left early when the night was still young, mayhap to be with their lovely Rosarios elsewhere.

This week, our paper carried pages from the past on the drug (opium) problem in the Philippines in the 1930's when our Guv-Gen was Chester Davis (the famed and coveted Davis Cup in tennis was named after him). At this time, we note how ancient the drug problem is and there are reports on how vicious Fentanyl could be. Prez Digong acknowledges using it as a pain-killer. It is also a people-killer. See "Fentanyl kills 16 in English city," Phil. Star, Feb. 5, 2018, p. 15, col. 5. So careful, Mr. Prez, we wish you well and pray that you change in some ways, and succeed, "for our good and the good of all His church [our people]".

The Manila Times of February 3, 1930, p.1 (page or blast from the past), as reprinted here last Saturday, recounted that a League of Nations Opium Mission arrived that morning, to "interfere, " what else? The body was composed of two Swedes, a Belgian, a Czech and a Brit. The party was met on board by a PC Colonel, who did not denounce the interference, and in fact brought the party to Malacañang. Today, Digong and Bato de la Rosa would tell a similar mission where to go. Not to

China, where shabu (worth billions) apparently continues to come, through our porous shorelines.

Guv-Gen Davis placed at the visitors' disposal the government's facilities for assistance. It had been formed at the instance of the British government and its ultimate purpose was to help devise legislation to lessen the evils of drug trafficking. The commission had visited ten places and would visit five more and thence to Geneva about the middle of April 1930. That night, Davis gave a Palace banquet in honor of the commission dealing with a long-time problem. Ambeth Ocampo wrote in the Inquirer in April 2016 that Rizal tried Mary Jane (marijuana).

As I also said here in 2016, Tibo Mijares wrote in the Conjugal Dictatorship: "[Y.S.] Kwong made the stunning revelation that Josefa Edralin [Macoy's Ma] was arrested in Arellano High School for having opium and heroin in her possession. Kwong even mentioned the name of the arresting officer as Telesforo Tenorio, then a detective but later . . . a chief of police of Manila. The suspicion was that Josefa was selling drugs to the students of the school where she was a teacher and librarian. According to Kwong, Josefa was able to either bribe or cry her way of out the incident." Page 257.

Speaking of American Guv-Gens, we also should recall at this time of year Frank Murphy, as we mark Manila's liberation in February 1945. After him was named what is now known as Camp Aguinaldo. Murphy was the last U.S. Guv-Gen here, the last one, as a Justice, I would have thought would take the side of Yamashita when his case reached the U.S. Supreme Court. I emotionally and heatedly blasted Yamashita in our class in Harvard

Law in 1967-68, to my classmate' resounding approval - they applauded; it took me decades to realize the wisdom of not succumbing to the high feelings of the moment for in the sober afterglow we may realize the sorry implications of emotionalized Fire!Aim!Ready! crusades. This I seem to see in the current Dengxavia controversy. Clint Eastwood' s sage advice is for one to know his limitations. Medical expertise is not universal, on autopsies, a distinct specialty.

Last Tuesday, I saw here a pix of Mayor Erap Estrada and Veep Leni Robredo marking the Liberation of Manila, a bloody month-long (Feb. 3 to Mar. 3, 1945) episode in which 100,000 were killed south of the Pasig. Admiral Sanji Iwabuchi (when defeat was imminent, he committed suicide, said in Japan to be the sincerest form of apology; unknown here, masakit yata) was in command of 12,000 Marines. But, it was Tomoyuki Yamashita, who had lost communication and control over his 4,000 soldiers, who was executed; he was up north in the bloody month-long battle. It gave rise to the controversial Yamashita Standard of command responsibility. That may also be the Nuremberg Standard, thanks to Hitler.

But getting more and more widespread is the use of the Hitler-Duterte salute, with fists thrust forward. This was standard and expected of Hitler's storm troopers, the reason Aussie Spymaster Nick Warner got pummeled and pilloried from pillar to post for doing the fist bump with Digong. Our own people are either too scared or too ignorant not to to be lemmings. Fellow Bedans are ignorant?

Anyway, a son told me last Tuesday San Beda is now a university.(?) When I entered San

Beda, in 1955, a promdi from Pasig, it was but a small college, but like Daniel Webster, speaking of Dartmouth, I say, there were those of us who loved it, and always will.

There I learned much about fierce Muslim warriors who never submitted to Imperial Manila; this may be an argument why there is martial law in Mindanao, and always will, or should, according to the Supreme Court, if I read correctly its latest excrescence, from where I sit, as a fervent student of human rights.

Saguisag & Associates Lawyers 4045 Bigasan Street, Palanan 1235 Makati Office Nos. (+632) 551-6350 <+63%202% 20551%206350> /833-4140 Fax No. (+632) 831-2276 <+63%202% 20831%202276>

oooooo

17

Lack of Inter-Branch Courtesy; Answering to History

Rene Saguisag
Nov 9, 2017, Manila times opinion

As spokesperson of then candidate Cory Aquino in 1985-86, it was a pleasant task for me to announce that Manang Letty Ramos-Shahani, then in the foreign service, had come out openly in support of our candidate, in defiance of the dictator. Then came the equally public and bold defection of Col. Mariano Santiago, a hero in Edsa'86. I was reminded of him because his brother, General Dionisio had just resigned/retired or fired as PDEA chief. Running in the family is high principle, at stake in a pending impeachment proceeding.

I endorsed another candidate for Chief Justice (CJ) in 2012, not Associate Justice Meilou Sereno. But, the President' s call was for her, which was legit and totally in order. So unlike the gross post-midnight appointment of her predecessor, which called for institutional correction, by the people, thru their Representatives, done via impeachment, and by their Senators, via conviction and removal.

Now, courtesy seems to be in very short supply in this mal-administration. So bastos! La cortesia no quita la valentia, the Palace should remember. Courtesy does not detract from valor.

Every Justice, among many many others, has his moist eye cast on the Chief Justiceship, so I can understand the seeming lack of intramural support. But, it is not only the institution but the country itself at stake.*

I am incredulous at the rate Harry Roque arguably appears to be self-destructing. For him, and not say, remarkable Sal Panelo, to say CJ Meilou must resign so as not to damage the Supreme Court, sounds bizarre. What about the damage to the country' s institutional arrangements by such egregious lack of inter-departmental courtesy?

So, here's another stone, from where I sit, but I rightly don't know whether Harry will go to a hollow block factory or a bakery. Santa banana! Not satisfied with speaking for the Philippines, he now seems to speak also for China and its intentions. By what authority naman kaya? If he can really speak for China, he might find some way for it to stop exporting shabu to the Philippines. We watch what others do, not what they say. Does China really insist on using its labor force in its infrastructure projects here with our high unemployment? While making us stop doing what we want in our very own?

Even more, or equally, startling is UP Manila's opposition to medical marijuana, echoing the Philippine Medical Association. They may assume that the U.S., Canada, and many countries in South America and Europe are insane not to oppose marijuana. Bill Clinton, Dubya Bush and Barack Obama all flirted with Mary Jane, which may explain why Bill, as sexual predator, later romanced Moooannniiicccaa Lewinsky.*

What an individual does to destroy himself, with marijuana, the state would take over, by imprisoning, in some stinking overcrowded jail, and stigmatizing, a user, for life or a loooong time.

Portugal has decriminalized all drugs and sees users as sick frail people to be saved and rehabbed, not criminals to be destroyed by a prison record. But, things seem normal enough there. After an initial spike in use 15 or so years ago, it went down. And I have friends who went to Fatima last month, to mark the centennial of our Lady's Apparition in Portugal. Antonio Guterres is the new SecGen of the UN, where its General Assembly Special Session on drugs is moving towards liberalization.

Our Catholic Church supports medical marijuana use to deal with suffering.

Decriminalizing should kill the syndicates because the state will supply for free, or at nominal cost, in rehab facilities what syndicates charge in humongous sums. Kill the profit motive and kill trafficking.

China can prove its friendship by knocking off its shabu supply source. A small price to pay for our virtual dishonorable surrender of West Philippine Sea.

Last Tuesday, San Sebastian surrendered honorably to San Beda. I got to watch the game for all the NCAA semifinal marbles at the Mall of Asia Arena. Initially, I was seated at the Baste side. I had on a yellow shirt (Baste's color) and a red jacket**** (San Beda's). Then I was moved to courtside.

San Beda outlasted San Sebastian, which fought gallantly, and the Lions will now face the Lyceum juggernaut.*

I missed our Indian Yell that whips the blood and our former rousing Victory Song. I still feel antsy as to why the losers are made to stay on court and sing. They should be allowed to go at once to their locker room, and let alone to weep, in privacy.

Attendance was all right last Tuesday but the title series which begins today, in Araneta, another planet which is farther, and I cannot go to, I fear. I live in Palanan and the other night, for a meeting in Conti's in Greenbelt, nearly two hours it took me. This is where the administration's Kill-Pa-More policy may be needed, which seems to be overdoing it in the messy bloody and failed drug war. Take-Prisoners- for-Rehab will do.

No incident, much less a rhubarb or donnybrook, marred last Tuesday' s NCAA offering. Commissioner Bai Cristobal and the three refs deserve kudos. Two years ago, when San Beda lost to Letran, 82-85, in overtime. in the final game, the Three Blind Mice didn't see a lane violation with seconds to go. But, that's all right. San Beda owes it to one and all to remind them from time to time that it is not the only team in the league.

And Robert Bolick, like Jerry West in the 1970 NBA Finals, made an even longer shot from the foul line, a buzzer-beater, last Tuesday; without it, the score would have been a close 73-71. More than worth the price of admission. (OK, I had a free ducat.)

Looming is another Thrilla.

PNoy is charged in the Sandiganbayan for Mamasapano, an operation that bagged Marwan, who had at least $5M on his head. No one runs for Prez claiming perfection and infallibility. Else, only the likes of Bedan Justice Gregorio Perfecto would qualify. When troopers go to enemy lair, particularly Morolandia, they knew some would come back in boxes.

Kennedy and the Bay of Pigs, Johnson and the Tet Offensive, Carter and the Iran rescue, Reagan and the Marines in Beirut, the Bushes and Obama in Iraq, and Clinton in Black Hawk Down, might have erred and misjudged, but with no personal gain. To err is human.

And like Fidel Castro, proclaim, "la historia me absolvera!" History will absolve me, PNoy can say. Indeed, the like the American Presidents, he should not have even been charged.

There is no talk even of going after those who killed comrades in fatal friendly fire in Marawi. Nor of why Digong was in Russia when the Marawi bloodletting began. And rightly so even if military intelligence again surfaced as a seeming contradiction in terms. Sino po ang mga natulog sa pansitan, resulting in having to destroy Marawi in order to save it? Like Vietnam' s Ben Tre?

Graft in PNoy's situation is hard to fathom. Usurpation? What, pray tell, is a Prez and Commander-in- Chief, prohibited from doing within his executive domain?

Saguisag & Associates Lawyers 4045 Bigasan Street, Palanan 1235 Makati Office

oooooo

18

Di Po Pederalismo and Problema, Kundi Kayo Mismo

Rene Saguisag
On Thu, Aug 9, 2018, Yahoo Account

Senator Ping Lacson impishly said that his chamber is ready to cremate whatever Cha Cha cadaver the Bigger House may send to the Better House, Frankfurter&# 39;s "derelict upon the waters of the law" if I may mix my metaphors.

What made the Consultative Committee (Conscom) spokesman tap Mocha Uson to sell its Draft? That she could seduce the populace the way she apparently did candidate and now Prez Digong? Was it because there is a CHA in her name, as in MO-CHA for CHA CHA?

"Ginoong Pangulo at Binibining Mocha, di po sistema ng pamahalaan ang problema, di po Pederalismo, kundi po, kayo mismo!"

A hard sell. She was reportedly approached to help lead the campaign to promote its Draft, on the initiative of the Conscom spokesman, who may or may not have clearance from it.

Permit me to doubt the wisdom of the move, validating that we are decaying in more than one front. Indeed, in what aspect of government are we better off today than we were when I was a law student and a young lawyer in the 50's and 60's? Are we a failed democracy?

It seems a truly serious YES campaign should be led by, among others, Chief Justice (CJ) Rey Puno, Senator Nene Pimentel, Vic de la Serna and Rudy Robles, topnotch lawyers; the latter three were elected ConCon Delegates in 1971. Fr. Rannie Aquino is a jurisprudence scholar or pundit.

But, what about the dismal aspect of economics?

Can they point to any tree with money growing on it?

In 1986-87, I, as Cory, Jr., was among those who led the campaign for the ratification of the Cory Constitution (now sought to be replaced by the Mo-CHA version). Walk in the park. But, it was the song, not the singer. Easy to sell the work of a body led by Justice Ka Celing Muñoz Palma as ConCom President, with Senator Ambo Padilla as Veep, aided by Chief Justice Berting Concepcion, and many others whose patriotism and sagacity were beyond a peradventure.

Thereby was killed the 1973 Constitution. 1971 ConCon and 1986 ConCom Delegate Pepe Nolledo narrated that in 1973, Barangay Assemblies were supposedly held. Asked who wanted Siopao, the attendees raised their hands, which were then marked as Yes votes.

Manny Pacquiao, on the other hand, is pushing for the anti-poor death penalty. All the statistics show that the rich boy flies, the poor boy fries. Extrajudicially killed, the poor may now be judicially murdered. The law represents the biases of the ruling class. Manny should consider the poor from whose ranks he came.

Snake oil salespersons we seem to see all over.

Now comes my pal, Ferdie Topacio, a celebrity lawyer with a celebrity client I chanced upon last Monday in the Sandiganbayan cafeteria. Ferdie, who flatters and flattens me by calling me Lodi, I again met the other evening in St. Luke's in the Fort. He was accompanying his ailing mother (not necessarily buying the facility). I learned about his presence because a waiter said he had picked up the tab, for us, unbidden.

Ferdie has helped put up a bounty for the heads of Ka Satur Ocampo, Liza Maza, Paeng Mariano and Teddy Casiño. The latter I met over dinner last July 24. I recall that Joker P. Arroyo would advise our detained national security clients, prisoners of conscience, that their first duty is to escape.

Ka Satur, et al., ingat, I don't know where any of you may be found; if I did, I ain't telling. But, if Ferdie raises the ante, I just might yield; Oscar Wilde said: "I can resist everything, except temptation."

Seriously, given that their alleged crime was supposedly committed about a dozen years ago, how I wish the Supreme Court could have found a way just to dismiss the case for the denial of the human and constitutional right to a speedy disposition of the case. So many years and not even first base we have reached, a very sad affirmation of Hamlet's "law' s delay." Inordinate delay indeed.

Lenny Villa was killed in an Aquila Legis hazing incident on February 11, 1991. Thanks to then Associate Justice Meilou Sereno, she finally decided the case on February 1, 2012. Among those acquitted was my client, Zos Dizon. On a motion for reconsideration, it was only in April 2016, when we got the ruling denying the motion, again, thanks to hardworking CJ Meilou. Actually, Zos, convicted by a Regional Trial Court, was acquitted twice by the Court of Appeals and twice by the Supreme Court! Multiple jeopardy and acquittals.

Going back to public hanging by the neck till dead, which the Prez prefers, what Manny Pacquiao should study is whether in its application, the death penalty has been anti-poor, the ranks from which he came. Taksil po sa kanyang kauri? **The rich criminals are probably in the corridors of power.**

The law represents the biases of the ruling class.

Manny and Tito Sotto should study the Portuguese experience and the UN General Assembly Special Session on Drugs. Portugal sees druggies as sick, who should be rehabbed, not as gun-grabbing criminals to be destroyed in our horrid prison system. By decriminalizing ALL drugs, the syndicates would wither and die, as government would supply the drugs. No rise in drug use in Portugal. In fact, it is going south.

Public hanging represents the best thinking of centuries ago. In England pickpockets would ply their trade while a hanging went on. We should not add judicial murder to extrajudicial killings. An eye for an eye, a tooth for a tooth, rape the rapist?*

Not only Manny Pacquiao has read the Bible. So also has the Pope. So have I, the Jerusalem Bible, cover to cover, from the Old Testament of Lamech, to Lex Talionis - to the New, which teaches compassion and forgiveness.

Do we prefer decay in values? Certainty and swiftness of conviction deter, not the severity of the penalty. A criminal does not carry a copy of the penal code and looks at what he can afford, a discredited supermarket theory of the criminal laws *> * Last Friday night, in a birthday party, someone sang Vincent (Starry Starry Night). Senator Vincent Sotto should play and listen to the song with its haunting melody.

MABINI's Alex Padilla, of La Salle and UP, sang and danced in a party of Bedans whose BoyNing Suzara was marking a birth anniversary.

Bogs Bonifacio' s emailed invite had said Alex would sing MacArthur Park. He delivered. Bobby Mondejar, a friend of the bday boy, sang, with feeling, Vincent (Starry Starry Night), part of whose lyrics were emblazoned on a wreath in the wake of hero/martyr Dr. Bobby de la Paz in Malate in 1982. A few nights ago I watched on TV a film on Vincent Van Gogh's life. And very briefly last Tuesday early in the morning, MacArthur, starring Gregory Peck.

Dr. Sylvia was Dr. Bobby's widow I got to meet after my unsayable loss of 2007. The one we suspected to have been behind Bobby's salvaging, I got to know when my wife and I were dancexercising in Intercon. Col. F would wait in the coffee shop below and drank, while his wife also dancexercised in Bahia.

Music and dance have the power to make us happy in this vale of tears. Like meeting top showbiz types. Celebrities.

I met Joan Baez in Prez Cory's 1986 San Fran visit; earlier I met Sigourney Weaver in New York. In 1996, my wife and I saw Linda Ronstadt in Las Vegas and Blue Bayou alone was more than worth the cost of admission.

We need to relax to keep what is left of our sanity. "Now I understand what you tried to say to me, and how you suffered for your sanity, how you tried to set them free, they would not listen, they did not know how, perhaps they'll listen now, starry, starry night."

Here's hoping Digong and Mocha will listen to the people now.*

I cannot close without remarking that pepe I associate with Pepe and Pilar, Rizal, Nolledo and Ka Pepe Diokno, souls of decency. As a Tagalog only now am I told that it could be linked to toxic indecency. That's rich. Pekpek, let's stick with, and continue to link pepe with what is edifying. We all have a stake in arresting decay in values, institutions and processes certain administration types appear to want to continue leading us.

Saguisag & Associates Lawyers 4045 Bigasan Street, Palanan 1235 Makati Office Nos. (+632) 551-6350/833- 4140 Fax No. (+632) 831-2276.

oooooooo